THE MORAL TEACHING OF PAUL

THE
MORAL
TEACHING
OF PAUL

VICTOR PAUL FURNISH

Abingdon
•
Nashville

THE MORAL TEACHING OF PAUL

Library of Congress Cataloging in Publication Data

FURNISH, VICTOR PAUL.
    The moral teaching of Paul.

    Bibliography: p.
    Includes index.
    1. Bible. N.T. Epistles of Paul—Ethics. I. Title.
    BS2655.E8F79   227'.06   78-10633

ISBN 0-687-27180-0

Scripture quotations, unless noted otherwise, are from the Revised Standard
Version Common Bible, copyright © 1973 by the Division of Christian
Education of the National Council of Churches.

Scripture quotations noted NEB are from the New English Bible. © the
Delegates of the Oxford University Press and the Syndics of the Cambridge
University Press 1961, 1970. Reprinted by permission.

MANUFACTURED BY THE PARTHENON PRESS AT
NASHVILLE, TENNESSEE, UNITED STATES OF AMERICA

To

DOROTHY JEAN FURNISH

sister
teacher
colleague

Contents

Preface **9**
   I. The Sacred Cow and the White Elephant **11**
  II. Sex: Marriage and Divorce **30**
 III. Homosexuality **52**
 IV. Women in the Church **84**
   V. Christians and the Governing
        Authorities **115**
Index of Scripture Passages **142**

Preface

This book is written for people who believe that Paul's moral teaching ought to be taken seriously but who are not sure what it means to do so. I have outlined my own convictions about this in chapter 1. In the subsequent chapters, I have sought to demonstrate how some problem texts in Paul's letters can still give moral guidance in our time if we do not force our presuppositions and questions upon them too quickly.

I was encouraged to move ahead with the publication of these short studies by the need, expressed to me often by laypeople, clergy, and students, for sound but nontechnical discussions of these problem texts and topics in Paul's letters. It is for such readers that this book is intended. Several of the chapters have been shaped in no small part by opportunities I have had to discuss these issues in the seminary classroom, at pastors' conferences, and in local churches. Many technical matters have been omitted from the presentation; others have been greatly simplified but, I hope, not misrepresented. The books and articles referred to at the end of each chapter will provide additional information and in certain cases different opinions.

The writing of this book was worked into a schedule which my wife and daughters thought was already too crowded, and without their understanding and support it could not have been accomplished. The manuscript was typed by Mrs. Bonnie Jordan with her usual skill and efficiency.

I

The Sacred Cow
and the White Elephant

The apostle Paul has the unenviable distinction of having
been and remaining one of history's most controversial and
misunderstood figures. He was misunderstood, first of all, by his
own fellow Christians. His dramatic and unexpected conversion
from being a zealous persecutor of the church to claiming to be a
qualified apostle of Christ inevitably made him suspect to his
new Christian colleagues, as well as making him *persona non
grata* to his former colleagues in Judaism. As his mission to the
Gentiles increasingly took on momentum and importance, his
relationship to the Jerusalem leaders of the Jewish-Christian
church became tense and increasingly difficult. Similarly, to his
Gentile converts, he often posed a puzzle. How could he, on the
one hand, preach freedom from the law, and on the other hand
declare that the man or woman in Christ is placed under a yet
more total claim to do God's will than the Jews, committed to the
fulfilling of the law? In the decades after his death, even as his
letters were becoming a fixture in the Christian canon and as he
was being increasingly venerated as a person, he continued to
be misinterpreted and misunderstood. One indication of this is
the famous comment of the second-century author of II Peter
who complains of the Pauline letters that "there are some things
in them hard to understand, which the ignorant and unstable
twist to their own destruction" (3:16).

In the late nineteenth and early twentieth century, it was

11

especially Paul's theology, even more specifically his preaching of Jesus as the Christ, that came under attack by liberal Protestants. The Apostle was portrayed as having, more or less single-handedly, converted "the religion of Jesus" into "a religion about Jesus." Some claimed Paul had infused the simple faith of the Nazarene and his disciples with alien concepts drawn from the Greek philosophical schools and the Eastern mystery cults. Others believed he had imposed on it the burden of rabbinic concerns and methods. The German scholar William Wrede once dubbed Paul "the second founder of Christianity," and lamented that, while Jesus' teaching had exerted "the better" influence on Christianity, Paul's had exerted "the stronger."

Subsequent investigations into the origins of Christianity have shown how naïve it was to label Paul the founder of Christianity as we know it; Paul was converted by and into a Christian movement that already had a rich theological tradition and that had already been nurtured by various religious and cultural sources. Paul made his own theological contributions, to be sure, but the church before him had received its initial and decisive momentum from the recognition by the earliest community that the Jesus who had been crucified lived among them still, as its risen Lord.

Although one may still hear echoes of the old complaint about the "corrupting" influence of Paul's theology on Christianity, at the present time it is more especially his *ethical teachings* that have been thrown into question. While the older, "liberal" view of Paul emphasized his dogmatic interests and argued that all else was subordinate to them, even Wrede had to acknowledge that Paul's ethical interests were also considerable. The Apostle is by no means shy in laying down practical admonitions and exhortations in his letters. He is often bold and blunt in the directions he gives, in the advice he offers, in the opinions he expresses. And so it was, for example, that he had sent Timothy to Corinth to remind the Christians there of all the Apostle's "ways in Christ, as I teach them everywhere in every church" (I Cor. 4:17). What are we to do with these today? The general appeals present no special problem; we may not agree *what* "love" requires in a given instance, but we can agree readily enough *that* we should "make love [our] aim" (I Cor. 14:1), "bear one another's burdens" (Gal. 6:2), and "hold fast what is good, abstain from every form of evil" (I Thess. 5:21). But we begin to have problems whenever Paul's admonitions become specific and concrete, as they so often do: men should not wear long hair (I Cor. 11:14), and women should (I Cor. 11:15); one should not use the secular courts (I Cor. 6:1 ff.); one should accept the social status (for example, slavery) in which one finds oneself (I Cor. 7:17 ff.); it is better to remain single than to marry (I Cor. 7:7a); and many more. How are we to understand these concrete instructions? In what way, if at all, are they applicable to us in our day?

Subsequent chapters will examine several topics of special current interest on which Paul's letters offer concrete advice and instruction. However, it is important first of all to be aware of a fundamental issue that confronts anyone who seeks guidance from the Bible in matters of conduct. The issue, at base, is one's understanding of the nature and authority of the Bible. It is clear that the church has recognized the Bible as authoritative for its faith and life. Unfortunately, Christian people have not always agreed on *how* the Bible's authority should be understood, particularly in its concrete teachings about morality. This important topic cannot be treated fully here, but some fundamental points must be established right at the start so that the subsequent discussions of specific issues can be of maximum benefit. At the risk of caricature, but for the sake of clarity, one may contrast two very different ways Paul's concrete moral teaching has been approached. There are some who venerate it as a sacred cow, and others who dismiss it as a white elephant.

As each of these positions is characterized, and the errors in each identified, it will become clear that the approach in the following chapters can be identified with neither.

Paul's Moral Teaching as a Sacred Cow

Some people believe, or at least read the Bible as though they believed, that scripture is the written deposit of God's truth, mediated through inspired writers in centuries past, but valid in both general and specific ways for all times and places. This may be called the sacred-cow view of the Bible. It leads to the conclusion, when applied to the concrete ethical teachings of Paul, that they are in fact God's commandments and thus eternally and universally binding. They are not to be touched, disturbed, or in any sense explained away. They are to be taken at face value. Proponents of this view of the Bible, and of Paul's letters specifically, often quote II Timothy 3:16: "All scripture is inspired by God and profitable for teaching, for reproof, for correction, and for training in righteousness." This text is offered as "proof" that the teachings of the Bible are of divine origin exclusively, and therefore in no way conditioned by the cultural setting of the biblical writers. It would seem to follow, then, that if we are uncomfortable with, for example, the teaching in Paul's letters about slavery or hairstyles or subjection to earthly rulers, that is *our* problem, not the Bible's. Since Paul's words are really God's Word, Christians have no business trying to accommodate them to modern views. Rather, Christians must accommodate *themselves,* by obeying those teachings as the commandments of God.

The fundamental problem with this way of approaching the Bible, and Paul's ethical teaching within it, is the fact that such an approach seriously misrepresents the understanding and intentions of the biblical writers themselves. It is true that the Old Testament prophets, for example, had uttered their oracles as spokesmen for God. But it is also true that those same Old Testament prophets were addressing God's Word to particular situations, and that they understood its applicability within a specific span of time and a particular geographical area. Neither they, nor those who later compiled their oracles and committed them to writing, presumed that the prophets' words could be isolated from the particularities of the situations in which they were originally spoken.

But then what of the text from II Timothy 3:16, quoted so often in defense of a sacred-cow conception of the Bible? To begin with, one must acknowledge a grammatical ambiguity that, in addition to the translation quoted above, permits the alternative found in the RSV footnote: "Every scripture inspired by God is also profitable for teaching, . . ." On this reading the emphasis is not that *all* scripture *is inspired* by God, but that every scripture that is inspired "*is profitable* for teaching, for reproof, for correction, and for training in righteousness." It is also probable that the "scripture" mentioned here means only the *Jewish* scripture, our Old Testament. But most important of all, one must admit that the critical word "inspired" is left vague and unspecific. Only persons can be "inspired," properly speaking, not an inanimate object like a written document. It is already a metaphorical use of the term to apply it to scripture. In and of itself the adjective "inspired" says only that those who have written these words were in some way moved and guided by God. Neither it, nor the equally general term "profitable" (that is, something "helpful" or "advantageous"), requires one to think of scripture as infallible, entirely unaffected by the cultural settings in which the writers labored, wholly consistent, or unconditionally binding for all times and places.

This is confirmed with special clarity in the instance of the Pauline letters. It is important to recognize that Paul was not conscious of contributing to scripture, of writing words that would be read and studied for generations, even centuries to come. He was not writing for us. He was writing to specific Christian congregations, in specific locations, involved in specific situations, at specific times. Since we are *not* the readers Paul had in mind, we must *interpret* his letters, including his moral instructions. They cannot possibly be automatically, and without remainder, applicable to us in our situations. One may speak of Paul's ministry, and therefore of his instructions, as "inspired," but this does not alter the fact that those instructions were meant for others and that what was pertinent in their times and places may not be in ours.

Willi Marxsen has offered a good illustration to make this point. Suppose that Paul sat down to write to the Galatian Christians and to the Thessalonian Christians at the same time (which, of course, was not actually the case). And suppose further that when he addressed the packets in which the letters had been placed for delivery, he mistakenly wrote "To the Thessalonians" on the letter intended for Galatia, and "To the Galatians" on the letter intended for the Thessalonians. What would have happened when the Thessalonians, between whom and Paul there were strong and mutual bonds of love and affection, opened up the letter addressed to them and found the angry and sarcastic words Paul had intended for the Galatians? And what would have happened among the churches of Galatia when they discovered that they had mistakenly been given Paul's letter to the Thessalonians? Now, certainly, the Thessalonian and Galatian Christians had much more in common with each other than we have with either group; and yet in both the churches of Galatia and in the congregation at Thessalonica a good deal of interpretive work would have had to be done in order to make those misdelivered letters intelligible and meaningful for the people. How much more are we in the position of needing to *interpret* Paul's letters, precisely because they were intended not for us, but for others.

An additional factor is that we are separated from Paul's

congregations geographically as well as in time. The socio-political-cultural conditions and problems of Paul's congregations are vastly different from the sociopolitical-cultural conditions and problems confronting modern Christians. The responsibilities and opportunities of our time and place are different from the responsibilities and opportunities of Christians in Paul's day. Paul was not writing "timeless truths" intended to be valid and relevant for all future ages. There are timeless truths to be found in his letters, but these are embedded within the particularities designed to be relevant to those whom he was addressing. We must remember that what made Paul's letters intensely relevant for his churches, serves to accentuate the differences between his day and ours, the differences between the needs of his original readers and our needs.

There is yet another reason why one must avoid making Paul's moral teaching into a sacred cow. Paul himself allows for differing ethical judgments, given the differing circumstances of individuals even within the same congregation and at the same time. He shows a sometimes amazing tolerance of rather differing behavior within the Christian communities. He accepts the fact, even affirms it, that some Christians will eat meat which has been ritually slaughtered in a pagan temple, while others will feel bound to abstain from it. He allows that some Christians will marry, while others will remain single; that some Christians will divorce, while others will maintain their marriages; and so forth. Some of these points will be examined in more detail later on. Here it is enough to emphasize that Paul nowhere lays down a rigid, legalistic code of Christian conduct. Taking his moral teaching as a sacred cow, therefore, simply will not work.

Indeed, if one looks beyond the Pauline letters to the New Testament as a whole, the variety of perspectives on practical issues is even greater. It is evident that the earliest church regarded neither its theological nor its ethical traditions as a sacred cow. Within the New Testament itself we see the church interpreting, reinterpreting, correcting, and modifying its traditions for new times and situations. Long before James Russell Lowell ever phrased it so eloquently, the earliest Christians, including Paul, recognized that "new occasions teach new duties; time makes ancient good uncouth." When one talks about the "traditions" in the early church, one should not picture sets of theological and ethical teachings tied up in neat packages, handed on from generation to generation with the warning, "Do not disturb." The theological and ethical traditions within the earliest church remained ever alive and growing; they were not allowed to stagnate and die. For all of his respect for traditions, including the ethical ones, Paul, for example, never confused those traditions, even those compiled into "scripture," with the gospel, the Word of God itself. He constantly reminded his churches, just as Jesus had constantly reminded his hearers, that God's living Word stands *over* and *in judgment upon* every tradition. God's Word is that by which every tradition is to be measured and judged. Whenever we make any of the traditions of the early church, including Paul's moral instructions, into a sacred cow, we are *embalming* the tradition rather than receiving it as a vital and revitalizing force—free to grow, free to develop and change, free to adapt itself to "new occasions and new duties."

Paul's Moral Teaching as a White Elephant

In view of what has been said here by way of criticism of the sacred-cow interpretation of Paul's ethical teachings, it might appear that the only alternative is to judge them to constitute a bulky white elephant. Webster reminds us that we use this phrase "white elephant" to refer to "anything requiring a great deal of care and expense, but yielding little profit; any burdensome possession." Go to any garage sale, and you will see numerous examples of white elephants! A white elephant is anything that is obsolete—perhaps once useful, but now outmoded, irrelevant, maybe even a little ridiculous.

All these terms—"outmoded, irrelevant, ridiculous"—have been applied to Paul's moral teaching. It too, some say, is an imposing but nonetheless unprofitable and burdensome white elephant. Perhaps it was pertinent to other times and places, but no longer. It is an anachronism, like an antique automobile: interesting only to antiquarians, but a real menace when it is driven out onto a modern expressway.

Undoubtedly the most important complaint lodged against Paul's moral teaching by those who would call it a white elephant is this: Paul expected the imminent end of the world, the speedy return of Christ, the close of the age before his own physical death. Moral instructions conveyed in that setting cannot possibly be relevant in a world that no longer lives with that kind of expectation, and whose very existence shows that Paul was mistaken. This is such an important point that it deserves careful examination and response.

More than fifty years ago the great German New Testament scholar, Martin Dibelius, argued that the early Christian expectation of the imminence of the end of the world automatically precluded any serious concern for ethical behavior within the world in the short time that remained. Dibelius claimed that such moral instruction as did occur among the first-generation Christians was really only a kind of "left-over" from Christianity's Jewish heritage. Dibelius held that the earliest Christians, including Paul, were also influenced by Greek ethical teachings, and adopted many of these, along with the Jewish ideals. Then they "christianized" both kinds of materials only insofar as that was necessary. Therefore, in his view Paul's ethical teachings had "nothing to do with the theoretic foundations of the ethics of the Apostle, and very little with other ideas peculiar to him. Rather, they belonged to tradition." That is, in his concrete instructions Paul was simply drawing on the traditions of the church which had, in turn, been adapted from Hellenistic Judaism. In preaching to converts from a Gentile background, Christian missionaries like Paul found it necessary to convey such basic moral exhortation for purely practical reasons, and not because such exhortation was related in any essential way to the proclamation of the gospel. The ethical sections of Paul's letters, then, Dibelius claimed, are there only because of the "didactic habit" Paul had of giving ethical instructions to new converts. On this view, the Pauline ethical teaching is not only unrelated in any significant way to Pauline theology, it is in fact seen as having existed *in spite of* the early church's expectation of an imminent eschaton. And we are left with a white elephant.

An essentially similar conclusion was reached by Albert Schweitzer, but Schweitzer arrived at the conclusion in a different way. He argued that the real Paul is Paul the "mystic," that Paul's theology is oriented fundamentally to the idea of a "mystical" dying and rising with Christ. Paul's ethical teaching was developed, then, "solely from the character of the new state of existence which results from the dying and rising again with Christ and the bestowal of the Spirit." Schweitzer acknowledged that Paul regarded the end of history and of the world as imminent, and for this reason, he said, the idea of a coming judgment and reward still lingers in Paul's ethical teachings. Yet the essential character of Paul's ethics does not derive from the Apostle's expectation of the coming end of the natural world. Its *essential* character derives, instead, according to Schweitzer, from the experience of being in Christ. Paul's mysticism, according to his view, was more important than his eschatology; Paul's mysticism saved him from denying the world in the way that most of his contemporaries did. The "ideal of Paul's ethic," wrote Schweitzer, was "to live with the eyes fixed upon eternity, while standing firmly upon the solid ground of reality." In effect, Schweitzer was saying that Paul's ethical teaching is actually better than one would suppose it could be, considering his sense of standing near the close of history. The Apostle's eschatological doctrine was, in effect, overcome by his "mysticism" and by his "intuition." While Schweitzer admired Paul's ethical teaching, he nonetheless regarded it as existing *in spite of* the apostle's eschatology.

One of the most recent discussions of Pauline ethics, that by Jack T. Sanders, echoes several of these ideas, especially those of Dibelius. Thus, Sanders, too, argues that Paul's belief in the shortness of time left for this world has precluded his developing any significant ethical teachings of his own. Paul correctly understood that love (*agape*) is the power of the "new existence," says Sanders, but when, at the same time, he identified that new existence as fully present only in the future, he was rendering the love commandment essentially irrelevant for the present. So, it is claimed, when the Apostle is forced to deal with concrete moral cases, he must fall back on arbitrary legal pronouncements. In effect, this recent interpreter is saying that the concrete moral instructions of Paul should be regarded as a white elephant, as a costly curio without any real present value.

At first, this may appear to be a more reasonable assessment of Paul's ethical teachings than that which venerates them as if they were a sacred cow. There have been some respected scholars who have reached this conclusion, and it certainly avoids the error of interpreting timely instructions as if they had been offered as timeless truths. But there are also some fundamental errors with the white-elephant interpretation.

First, the evidence does not support the view that the expectation of an imminent end of the world and history precludes concern for ethical behavior in the present. The view of Dibelius and others that first Jesus, and then the earliest Christians following him, more or less perfunctorily espoused Jewish or Hellenistic, or Hellenistic-Jewish, morality and traditions, is too superficial a reading of the texts. Jesus' preaching of the nearness of the reign of God did not preclude or cause the subordination of practical ethical concerns, but accentuated the totality of the claim that the sovereign God makes on his people to love him and one another. Jesus' own ministry of compassion, love, and service within the family of God is integrally related to his eschatological message about the imminence of the kingdom. Its nearness brings a new urgency to the ethical appeal. Similarly, as I have tried to show elsewhere, the so-called ethical sections of the Apostle's letters are not loosely tacked on to the weightier, theological parts, as concessions to the practical needs of the less than ideal Christians in Paul's congregations (Dibelius). Rather, Paul's ethical admonitions are closely and significantly related to his preaching of the gospel, and thus to his fundamental theological convictions. What matters most, he insists, is *faith enacted in love* (see Gal. 5:6), and by this he means (as the context of Galatians 5–6 clearly shows), *in the present life of the believer and of the believing community.* Virtually all of the Apostle's concrete moral instructions are intended to show the forms that faith's enactment in love must take in specific cases.

It is true that Paul does occasionally issue fairly arbitrary pronouncements on matters of behavior, what Sanders, following Ernst Käsemann, calls "tenets of holy law." These usually involve some warning about the visitation of God's judgment upon those who fail to keep them. In such passages (for example, I Cor. 3:17; but they are not as numerous as Sanders would have us believe), Paul does seem to be influenced by the form and content of traditional modes of exhortation. But one ought not to isolate such sentences from the wider context of Paul's ethical teaching. They are only elements embedded within larger units of teaching, and a fair appraisal of the relation between eschatology and ethics in Paul's thought can only result when the broader contexts are considered.

First Thessalonians, probably the earliest letter of Paul's we possess, offers a good illustration of the way his eschatological expectation actually supports his ethical appeals. In chapters 4 and 5, the eschatological hope is keen and vivid. The Apostle is very much concerned here with the future, the destiny under God, of believers. It is also clear in these chapters that Paul believes the decisive eschatological event has occurred already for them in the death and resurrection of Jesus Christ (see 5:10). Paul is saying that, whether the End is upon them or delayed for a little while, the most important thing for the Thessalonians is to know that they belong to the New Age. In Christ, by their faith in him, they are God's people. In certain paragraphs in these chapters, Paul is drawing very heavily upon traditional eschatological pictures he has inherited from Judaism. But when all is said and done, he describes the Christian's future in virtually the same way he talks about the Christian's present experience of being in Christ: "and so we shall always be with the Lord!" (4:17c), that is, "live with him" (5:10). The future for which one hopes is in its essential meaning nothing other than what is already given, a being "with Christ." Paul does not leave us guessing about the ethical implications of this, either. In I Thessalonians 5:5 he points out that the expectation of the Lord's return marks out Christians as "sons of light and sons of the day; we are not of the night or of darkness." Since we belong to the future, we are not ultimately "of this world." Then immediately, without pause or apology, Paul draws the practical ethical conclusion: "So then let us not sleep, as the others do, but let us keep awake and be sober" (vs. 6).

Another outstanding example of this, and one to which we shall return in a later chapter, is to be found in Romans 12–13. This long section of ethical appeals is prefaced in 12:1-2 and concluded in 13:8-14 with eschatological references. "Do not be conformed to this age [RSV footnote], but be transformed . . ."; "The night is far gone, the day is at hand. Let us cast off the

23

works of darkness and put on the armor of light; let us conduct ourselves becomingly as in the day, not in reveling and drunkenness," and so on. In still another letter, to the Philippians, Paul climaxes his admonitions with the reminder that believers are citizens of a heavenly commonwealth, from which they await their Savior, the Lord Jesus Christ (3:20). Their status does not undercut, but makes more urgent, their present ethical responsibilities. There is not, in fact, a major block of ethical teaching anywhere in the Pauline letters in which the practical appeals are not specifically and emphatically supported with reference to the hope by and in which the believer lives, and by and in which the believer has been granted his or her new identity as one "in Christ."

The Role of the Spirit

The interrelationship of Paul's eschatological expectation and his concrete moral instructions may be further clarified when one notes the way in which he sees the Holy Spirit functioning. When the Apostle speaks of the Spirit of God he is thinking primarily of the presence and power of God active in the life of the believing community and in the lives of those who are a part of it. Spatial metaphors tend to predominate in the way most of us think and speak of God and the Holy Spirit: God is "up there," and God's Spirit "comes down" to dwell among and in us. These spatial metaphors are certainly not alien to the Bible. But it is important to notice that Paul at least as often expresses the reality of God and of the Spirit in *temporal* metaphors, using, for example, the categories of present and future. On the one hand, he may conceive of the present moving ahead toward the future (for example, Rom. 13:11-12); and, on the other hand, he may conceive of God's future moving in on the present. In the latter case he writes of the Holy Spirit as the bearer of God's future, establishing the power of the New Age already in the

24

midst of this present age, within the community of those who, by their faith in Christ, are participants in the new creation. This is the meaning of two special metaphors, both temporal in character, by which Paul describes the Holy Spirit.

One metaphor derives from Israel's practice of offering to God, at the annual Festival of the Harvest (or "of Weeks"), the first and presumably choicest portion of the yield. These *first fruits* were not the whole, but they represented and in an important sense embodied the whole, symbolizing that the entire harvest was God's gift and belonged to him. When, in Romans 8:23, Paul refers to believers as those "who have the first fruits of the Spirit," he is thinking of the Spirit as the power of salvation present already with believers, empowering and renewing and, even in the midst of the present age, establishing them in the hope for the full harvest that is to come (see verses 24-25).

Paul's other temporal metaphor for the Spirit derives from the world of business and commerce, and it appears twice in II Corinthians. In these instances the idea is of a *down payment* or *first installment.* "God," writes Paul, "has given us the Spirit as a guarantee" (5:5). Such "earnest money" is not the whole sum, but it represents the whole, and it establishes the credit of the one from whom it has come. Here again Paul is thinking of the gift of the Holy Spirit as the effective presence of God's power in the present—not the fullness of it, but no less the reality of it in the believer's life: "[God] has put his seal upon us and given his Spirit in our hearts as a guarantee" (1:22). This image, like the other, shows that the concept of the Spirit plays a key role in Paul's thinking about the present and the future. The Spirit is the bearer of the power of the New Age, inaugurated, but not yet fulfilled, in the present life of believers.

Now what has this to do with ethics? How does this conception help us understand the vital relationship that exists between Paul's eschatological expectation and his concrete moral instructions? The answer is clear when one recognizes that for Paul the power of the New Age is *love*—not just love in general, but *God's* love, the love through which God has created all that is, in which God wills that it be sustained, and by which God acts to redeem it. For Paul the decisive *event* of God's love is Christ's death. There he finds established that powerful, redeeming love by which the world is reconciled to God and by which those who have faith participate in the new creation (II Cor. 5:14-20; Rom. 5:6-11). This is the love, *God's* love, to which faith is a response, and by which faith itself is empowered to express itself in the believer's life (Gal. 5:6, assuming a double reference in the verb: faith rendered active by God's love and expressed in the believer's love).

If Christ's death is for Paul the decisive *event* by which God's love is established, then it is equally true that for Paul it is God's Holy Spirit that is the decisive *bearer* of God's love, the means by which God's love is made present in the believer's life. "God's love," he writes in Romans 5:5, "has been poured into our hearts through the Holy Spirit which has been given to us." When this affirmation is added to the other cardinal points of Paul's preaching, one may begin to see how, finally, the Apostle's idea of justification by faith, his eschatological expectation, and his ethical concerns are all interrelated, even though he himself has nowhere worked the interrelationships out systematically. They are there, nevertheless, because he understands that faith is *only* faith as it is enacted in *love,* which is the power of the New Age present and active already in the Holy Spirit. It is therefore by the enlivening power of the Spirit that the believer is sustained and guided in his or her new life. "If we live by the Spirit, let us also walk by the Spirit," he writes to the Galatians (5:25), and in the same passage he has indicated that the principal (and all-inclusive) fruit of the Spirit is love (5:22). The three decisive marks of the life in Christ are faith, hope, and love, and of these it is love alone that never ends. That is so

26

because love is understood as God's power, the power of the New Age, reaching back into our present, claiming us for God and endowing our existence with meaning and direction.

Conclusion

It is unacceptable to treat Paul's moral instructions as if they were a sacred cow, and equally unacceptable to treat them as if they were a white elephant. It is not just that these ideas are too extreme, and that one must look for some middle way that will avoid the errors at both ends. Rather, these ideas are both *wrong.* The one approach, for which the sacred cow has been our symbol, misunderstands the nature of the Bible, the intentions of the biblical writers themselves, and the ways in which the moral instructions of Paul are related to the specific needs of Christians living in the Greco-Roman world. The other approach, symbolized here by a white elephant, fails to perceive the interrelationship that exists between Paul's proclamation of the gospel and his concrete ethical teachings and exhortations. In consequence of these points, before the meaning of Paul's moral teaching for our own day can be determined, its meaning for and in Paul's own day must be assessed. This requires that we pay attention both to the sociopolitical context in which Paul's ministry was conducted and to the broader context of Paul's preaching and ministry of which his moral teaching was an integral part.

One final observation about sacred cows and white elephants may help to clarify what is being argued here: *Whenever one treats Paul's moral teaching as if it were a sacred cow, one runs the risk of turning it into a white elephant.* That is, if we regard the particulars of Paul's moral instructions as automatically applicable and binding in *our* times and circumstances, we are sure to end up with a good many requirements that are either irrelevant or, what is worse, clearly inappropriate. Moreover, we shall be disappointed to find that Paul has nothing to say about problems that are real and urgent ones in the modern world: overpopulation and world hunger, nationalism, medical research and medical care, concern for the environment, to name a few. These are distinctively issues of the modern, technological age, and they must be faced and thought through even though no biblical writer could have addressed them in any specific way. But if we try seriously to understand and assess what Paul did have to say about the issues of his own day, how his teaching applied in the situations to which it was addressed, and how it functioned within the overall theological perspective of the Apostle, then it can take on new meaning for us in our day.

In the following chapters, attention will be focused on several topics that Paul discussed and that continue to be of concern for modern Christians. Even so, the principles enunciated above still apply. Just because the general *topics* are the same does not mean that the *issues* are the same. It must be our task to inquire, in each case, into the issues as Paul faced them and into the resources Paul had at hand as he responded to them. We should not expect to find clear and specific answers to our particular ethical questions. Paul's instructions were shaped to meet the situations that confronted him and his congregations in their world, and their relevance for Paul's first readers must be distinguished from their relevance for us. Their importance for us, as we shall see, is less in the particular patterns of conduct they promote than in the underlying concerns and commitments they reveal. They show us faith being enacted in love, and love seeking to effect its transforming power in the midst of this present age.

For Further Reading

A valuable book on the general topic of biblical ethics is *Bible and Ethics in the Christian Life,* by Bruce C. Birch and Larry L.

Rasmussen (Minneapolis: Augsburg Publishing House, 1976). Wolfgang Schrage's article, "Ethics in the New Testament," in *The Interpreter's Dictionary of the Bible,* Vol. 5 (Nashville: Abingdon, 1976), is especially helpful on Paul's teaching. On the topic of New Testament eschatology in general, see the article in the same volume by Elizabeth Schüssler Fiorenza. I have treated certain points in the foregoing chapter more extensively in *Theology and Ethics in Paul* (Nashville: Abingdon, 1968) and in a chapter on Paul in *The Love Command in the New Testament* (Abingdon, 1972). Robin Scroggs' *Paul for a New Day* (Philadelphia: Fortress Press, 1977) is a brief and useful introduction to the Apostle's teaching as a whole.

Books referred to or quoted in this chapter: William Wrede, *Paul,* trans. E. Lummis (London: Philip Green, 1907); Willi Marxsen, *The New Testament as the Church's Book,* trans. J. E. Mignard (Philadelphia: Fortress Press, 1972), an important discussion of the apostolic norm in the earliest church; Martin Dibelius, *From Tradition to Gospel,* trans. B. L. Woolf (London: Nicholson and Watson, 1934), especially pp. 238-39; Albert Schweitzer, *The Mysticism of Paul the Apostle,* trans. W. Montgomery (London: Adam and Charles Black, 2nd ed. 1953), quotations taken from pp. 297, 311, 333; and Jack T. Sanders, *Ethics in the New Testament* (Philadelphia: Fortress Press, 1975), chapter 3.

II

Sex: Marriage and Divorce

Among the most difficult and misunderstood passages in the Pauline letters are those which have to do with women, specifically with their role in marriage and their role in the church. On the one hand, there are those who fasten on these texts to prove how "unchristian" the movement for women's rights is. On the other hand, there are those who believe that in these matters, at least, the Apostle's personal biases were so substantial that his teaching can no longer be taken seriously. For this reason it will be important to examine that teaching with some care. In this chapter, only the question of marriage and divorce will be discussed; the issue of a woman's place in the church has been reserved for chapter 4.

Paul's principal comments on marriage and divorce occur in a passage, I Corinthians 7, where the fundamental issue is not the family, but whether sex ought to have any place in the life of a Christian. In Ephesians and Colossians there are passages that focus directly on the Christian household and the respective roles of husbands, wives, children, and slaves; but there are persuasive reasons for believing that those letters were written after Paul's death by a later interpreter of his teaching. It is precarious to base one's estimate of Paul's own teaching on those passages. (See below, pp. 89-91.) The place to begin is I Corinthians 7, where Paul is responding to some issues that have been raised by the Corinthians themselves.

The Situation in Corinth

The Corinthians have written to Paul asking for instruction on a series of matters which had stirred up controversy in their congregation. The Apostle refers to their letter in I Corinthians 7:1, and the remainder of his own letter is in response to it. In chapter 8 we see him dealing with the question of whether Christians should eat meat that has been ritually slaughtered in pagan temples. In chapter 11 the question concerns head coverings in church. In chapters 12–14 it is the question of spiritual gifts, in chapter 15 the future resurrection, and in chapter 16 the collection for the Christians in Jerusalem. But underlying all of these, including the question about sex discussed in chapter 7, is the belief, held apparently by a sizable number of Corinthians, that salvation has already been granted in its fullness. These Corinthians seem to have been ecstatics, convinced that they were gifted with a spirituality that in effect lifted them above the worldly and the physical. They probably regarded their speaking in tongues as one evidence of this, and perhaps they identified it with the language of the angels themselves (see I Cor. 13:1).

In I Corinthians Paul is more than once sharply critical of those who presume to possess a superior religious knowledge. " 'Knowledge' puffs up, but love builds up," he says (8:1). And in one of the most scathing indictments to be found anywhere in his letters, he caricatures these spiritually pretentious Corinthians by presenting them as claiming a status to which neither he nor any apostle could dare aspire: "Already you are filled! Already you have become rich! Without us you have become kings! And would that you did reign, so that we might share the rule with you!" (I Cor. 4:8). These naïvely arrogant Corinthians, claiming for themselves spiritual wisdom, knowledge, and glory, have missed the meaning of the cross. Such is the burden of Paul's message in the first four chapters of I Corinthians.

This special Corinthian brand of Christianity also had concrete moral implications. These were of two very different kinds. On the one hand, a view of salvation which, like the one Paul criticizes, demeans the worldly and physical, can lead to a reckless libertinism. If the spiritual existence is completely independent of the physical, then why be concerned about morality at all? "All things are lawful," must have been the libertinistic slogan of some of the Corinthian ecstatics. Paul quotes it back to them in I Corinthians 6:12 and 10:23 in order to correct it with the reminders, "but not all things are helpful" and "not all things build up." They were also saying, "Food is meant for the stomach and the stomach for food," by which they meant that being in Christ allows one to give free rein to all physical desires. This slogan, too, Paul quotes in order to refute. He warns: "and God will destroy both one and the other. The body is not meant for immorality, but for the Lord, and the Lord for the body" (6:12-13).

Other Corinthians, however, doubtless equally convinced of their superior religious status, were reading the ethical implications in quite a different way. They did not think that their special experience of salvation permitted them to give free rein to physical, worldly impulses and desires. They held that these must be denied, repressed, held in constant check. In matters of ethics they were not libertines but ascetics, especially in the matter of sex. The ascetics also had their slogans, and from Paul's standpoint the asceticism of this group was just as misguided as the libertinism of the other. It is above all the concern to correct the ascetic error that moves Paul to write to the Corinthians as he does about marriage and divorce.

Marriage

Paul's comments about marriage in I Corinthians 7 have been an embarrassment to many modern readers. One commentator has opined that "the best [Paul] can say for marriage in this entire chapter 7 is that it is no sin." And the same writer thinks the discussion reads like something that comes from a person who "had been through a marriage that almost but never quite succeeded." We shall see that these statements are not really fair to Paul.

To begin with, we must remember that Paul's topic is not marriage as such, but the place of sex in the Christian's life. Many recent commentators agree that quotation marks should be placed around the second half of verse 1, thus: " 'It is well for a man not to touch a woman.' " No such punctuation marks were available to Paul, so their inclusion or omission has to be an editorial decision of the translator. In I Corinthians 6:12, 13; 10:23, as noted above, the translators of the Revised Standard Version have seen fit to include them, indicating that Paul was quoting the Corinthians. That must also be the case in 7:1*b* (despite the RSV), otherwise the subsequent statements make no sense. The statement that a man should not "touch" (engage in sexual relations with) a woman is a slogan of the Corinthian ascetics. It was probably quoted to Paul in the letter sent to him from Corinth, along with the request that he give his authoritative opinion about its validity. This he proceeds to do at once (verses 2-7):

(2) Because of the temptation to immorality, each man should have his own wife and each woman her own husband. (3) The husband should give to his wife her conjugal rights, and likewise the wife to her husband. (4) For the wife does not rule over her own body, but the husband does; likewise the husband does not rule over his own body, but the wife does. (5) Do not refuse one another except perhaps by agreement for a season, that you may devote yourselves to prayer; but then come together again, lest Satan tempt you through lack of self-control. (6) I say this by way of concession, not of command. (7) I wish that all were as I myself am. But each has his own special gift from God, one of one kind and one of another.

33

Paul begins by affirming the traditional Jewish view of marriage: a husband shall have one wife, and a wife, one husband. The word here translated as "immorality" refers in particular to sexual immorality, and in effect the Apostle is emphasizing that apart from the covenanted relationship between a husband and a wife that marriage represents, sexual relationships are immoral. Paul's argument reflects the rabbinic teaching to which he was heir. The rabbis insisted on marriage for two main reasons. First, it was necessary for the purpose of procreation. Significantly, Paul does not use this argument. Because of his sense of living at the close of history, he could not have accorded such an argument any validity. But the rabbis also argued for the importance of marriage because without it one might be tempted by immoral forms of sexual activity. This argument does have meaning for Paul, and is doubtless echoed here in his phrase, "Because of the temptation to immorality."

Although Paul's response to the problem at Corinth has been influenced in part by one familiar rabbinic argument for marriage, that argument itself is not the Apostle's main point. It would be quite wrong to interpret either Paul or his rabbinic contemporaries as saying that marriage exists solely as an outlet for the sexual appetites. Such an interpretation is, in Paul's case, explicitly ruled out by his own sharp criticism of "the heathen" who enter into marriages precisely out of their "lust" (I Thess. 4:3b-5). Rather, the main point Paul wants to make is that sex is not only permissible (moral) within marriage, but is something due to each partner and therefore something for which each partner is obligated to the other. This is the point registered in verse 3, and it is one directed especially to the Corinthian ascetics, who were denying the propriety of sex for Christians under any conditions. They must have been arguing that the new life in Christ precludes a sexual union even between a husband and a wife.

In I Corinthians 6:15-16a Paul had reminded the Corinthians

about the incompatibility of membership in Christ's body and sexual union with a prostitute. This, again, was probably a standard part of his missionary teaching. Some Corinthians had misunderstood this to mean that *any* kind of sexual union defiles the temple of God, and thus the body of Christ. It is likely that they believed conversion to Christ required married persons either to separate or to maintain "celibate marriages." In the paragraph before us, however, we see Paul going on record as emphatically opposed to this view. The scriptural injunction of Genesis 2:24, which he had quoted in *opposition* to prostitution (I Cor. 6:16), would have led Paul just as readily to the *affirmation* of a sexual relationship between husband and wife: it is God's will that the two shall become "one flesh."

An outstanding feature of Paul's discussion in chapter 7 of I Corinthians is his emphasis on the need for a husband and wife to recognize their complete *mutual* responsibility in matters of sex (verses 3-4). One interpreter has called this an "incredible" and "repulsively external requirement," saying that "the mechanical sexuality envisioned for these marriages, is almost emetic in its conception." This is a gross distortion of Paul's meaning. His point is, first, that sex is a meaningful part of marriage, and meaningful only within marriage. And the second point is that neither partner should peremptorily thrust himself or herself upon the spouse in a way that would exploit the other person sexually. The statement about not ruling over one's own body (verse 4) is applied to *both* partners precisely in order to establish the point that *sex must be a shared relationship between two persons of equal standing.* What Paul is saying about mutuality in matters of sex (because sex is the issue being discussed here), he would say also about other aspects of the marriage relationship. This is shown by the important aside of I Corinthians 11:11, where, in a more general statement about the interdependence of male and female, he insists that "in the Lord woman is not independent of man nor man of woman."

In I Corinthians 7:5 Paul recognizes that sexual abstinence may have a place within marriage, but only under three conditions: that it be temporary, that it be by mutual agreement, and that it be for prayer. Otherwise, as in the more extreme case of celibate marriages, one may be tempted to seek the fulfillment of one's sexual desires elsewhere, and that would be immoral. It is probable that this allowance for temporary sexual abstinence within marriage is the "concession" (RSV) of which the Apostle speaks in verse 6, even though many have taken that as a reference to marriage itself. In either case, the word "concession" has come to have connotations in English that are not present in the Greek word Paul himself uses. We speak of a candidate "conceding" the election to an opponent, and our picture is of something reluctantly, maybe even bitterly acknowledged. But Paul's word connotes a different attitude, rather like "fellow-feeling" or "forbearance." It refers to an allowance made empathetically, out of concern, with constructive goodwill. So even if he does mean to say that marriage itself is allowed as a "concession," his point would be that it is allowed out of consideration for the well-being of those to whom it is permitted, and not just to be rid of their importuning.

Then what of verse 7, in which Paul expresses his wish that all were single as he himself is? (It is useless to speculate on whether he ever had been married; we have no evidence on the subject.) Doesn't verse 7 prove that Paul regards marriage as an inferior way of life for Christians? That the single state is his own preference is clear. It is equally clear, however, that he regards his celibacy as a "gift," and that this gift is not shared by all. Later in the letter he will tell the Corinthians that there are many diverse kinds of gifts, and that the possession of one or another is no reason for one member of Christ's body to claim pride of place over another—all the gifts are from the one Spirit (chapter 12). Whether or not Paul means to imply that the *married* Christian may also regard his or her status as a gift, he at least

36

does not flaunt his celibacy as proof of some superior religious or moral attainment. That would have played into the hands of the ascetics whose opposition to all sexual relationships he is anxious to correct.

It is often observed that Paul's teaching in this chapter of I Corinthians is conditioned in large part by his belief that "the form of this world is passing away" (verse 31 *b*). It is true that this sense of standing on the border between the old age and the new inhibits, if it does not actually preclude, a concern for the nature and quality of marriage as an ongoing social institution. What the times demand above all else, Paul believes, is single-minded devotion to "the affairs of the Lord," to the preaching of the gospel of Christ and the building up of his body into an authentic community of faith. Paul knows that marriage imposes special cares and responsibilities upon the partners—"worldly troubles," he calls them in verse 28. He wishes that Christians could be spared these in order to give their "undivided devotion to the Lord" (verse 35). A significant assumption underlies Paul's comments here. Committing oneself to a marriage means committing oneself in a special way to the existence of another by involving oneself with the spouse in a relationship of care and concern. It is significant that Paul does not *criticize* married persons for having anxieties and worldly cares. He accepts the fact that these are part of marriage. He is just thankful that he himself is not burdened with them. One might reasonably infer from this that, had Paul been writing about the responsibilities of marriage, he would have emphasized the caring that must be exhibited by both partners. Indeed, in verses 32-34 what is said of the man is also said of the woman; because marriage is a partnership, obligations run both ways. Mutuality and interdependence are again presumed.

Paul's sense of living at the close of the old age and at the dawning of the New Age also helps to explain the otherwise curious remark in verse 29 that "those who have wives [should] live as though they had none." By this he cannot possibly mean that Christians should eliminate sex from their marriages. That is the view in Corinth which he has been opposing. Nor can he mean that Christians should abandon the responsibilities normally associated with the married state. As we have seen, he presumes these must continue, and for that very reason he rejoices in his own gift of celibacy. The remark in question appears in a whole series of injunctions delivered in view of the "shortness" of the time (verses 29-31). Not only should those with wives "live as though they had none," but also "those who mourn as though they were not mourning, and those who rejoice as though they were not rejoicing, and those who buy as though they had no goods, and those who deal with the world as though they had no dealings with it." In none of these cases does Paul mean that the Christian should opt out of his or her worldly responsibilities. Earlier in this same letter, for example, he had chided the Corinthians for having mistakenly thought it was even *possible* "to go out of the world" (5:9-10). What he means in every instance is that no ultimate value is to be placed on worldly institutions or relationships. No mundane responsibility, however noble or important in this present age, should be allowed to make an *absolute* claim upon the Christian. The apostle is not denying the *importance* of the responsibilities worldly existence entails, but he is denying their *ultimacy.* Here, formulated with rhetorical skill, Paul is saying in effect that the Christian does not finally belong to this world, but exists within it, always under a higher claim.

Before moving on to what Paul writes to the Corinthians about divorce, we need to be aware of two special questions about marriage on which he comments. One of these questions pertains to Christians who once had spouses, but who have them no longer. Widows are mentioned specifically (verses 8-9 and 39-40). The other special question is about Christians who are pledged to each other, but whose marriages have not been consummated (verses 36-38). In each case, and consistent with his counsel to those who have never been married, Paul says it is preferable not to marry (or to consummate the marriage). Once more, however, he allows that marriage is better for those whose sexual feelings are strong (verses 9*a* and 36). The oft-quoted comment in verse 9*b*, "For it is better to marry than to be aflame with passion," has to be read in the context of Paul's whole discussion. One must remember that he regards celibacy as a *gift*. Considering the urgency of the present times, he regards it as the eminently more *practical* gift, but not as an inherently "superior" one. To espouse celibacy is no gain if it means to be tortured by strong, unfulfilled sexual desires. For such persons the married status is not just a poor "second best," but *the best;* for them it is the proper way in Christ. It is good, says Paul, to be married (verse 38*a*). The added comment that it is "better" not to be is prompted by his conviction that history is drawing to a close, that the responsibilities that are necessarily involved in marriage belong, like other worldly claims, to the realm of what have been called "preliminary concerns" (Paul Tillich), and that it is preferable for the Christian's fullest energies to be devoted "to the Lord." This is no disparagement of marriage. It is Paul's effort to cope with the realities of the present time as he understands them.

Divorce

The matter of separation or divorce from one's partner also claims Paul's attention in I Corinthians 7, presumably because it was another of the points in dispute among the Corinthian Christians. It is taken up in two different connections.

The topic arises first of all in verses 10-11: "To the married I give charge, not I but the Lord, that the wife should not separate from her husband (but if she does, let her remain single or else be reconciled to her husband)—and that the husband should not divorce his wife." It is significant that Paul says his authority for this teaching is "the Lord." This is one of the very few instances in his letters where the Apostle appeals directly to Jesus' teaching. (The other instances are in I Cor. 9:14 and 11:23 ff.; possibly also I Thess. 4:14-15.) We know that these teachings had been kept alive in the traditions of the church through their oral repetition and interpretation, as well as through their practical application. Finally, but not until after Paul's death, they were committed to writing. Jesus' teaching on divorce to which Paul is referring here has been preserved, although in different forms, in all three Synoptic Gospels, indeed twice in Matthew (Matt. 5:31-32; 19:9; Mark 10:11-12; Luke 16:18). Most commentators have argued that the Gospel of Mark (followed closely in the Gospel of Luke) has provided us the earlier form of Jesus' teaching, and that in the Gospel of Matthew one sees how the church softened that in the concrete application. On the face of it, this would appear to be the case, because the prohibition of divorce is apparently absolute and unconditional in Mark, while in both Matthean passages divorce "on the ground of unchastity" is allowed. It has also been held, however, that the exception-clause was an original part of the teaching. On this view, in Matthew 5 and Mark 10 the saying of Matthew 19:9 has been "abstracted" into a community regulation, and while in Mark permission for divorce "on the ground of unchastity" is not specifically indicated, it is nonetheless presumed. But the more immediate question for us is what Paul understands the requirements to be in this matter.

It was the Greco-Roman world of the first century that Paul knew, and in which Christianity emerged. In that milieu, marriages were just as easily dissolved as they were made in the first place. In society as a whole, no religious sanctions or ideals influenced very significantly either the making or breaking of marriages. Under Roman law, specifically, either husband or wife could initiate the divorce. Within Judaism, however, the

40

situation was different. There the marriage bond was regarded as profoundly important. The union of male and female was regarded as an essential ordinance of God, an integral part of God's creation. There was allowance for divorce, but only at the husband's initiative, not the wife's. By Jesus' day, usually only one reason for divorce was acknowledged, namely (as in Matthew) infidelity. And in practice, divorce seems to have been infrequent among the Jews.

The arresting thing about Paul's admonition in verses 10-11 is the apparent contradiction between the main point and the parenthetical remark. On the one hand he cites the Lord's command "that the wife should not separate from her husband . . . and that the husband should not divorce his wife." (It is not likely that any technical distinction between "separation" and "divorce" is intended; there is evidence from other ancient sources that the first term could mean "divorce" as well as the second.) On the other hand, Paul's aside presumes that separations will occur, and provides that when they do there should be no remarriage. If no reconciliation is possible, the woman, at least (perhaps also the man, although Paul does not say so explicitly), should remain single. Here the principle operates that it is better to be free to give one's undivided devotion to the Lord. Strong sexual feelings are not specifically provided for in verses 10-11, but Paul may have intended that what he had just written in this regard about "the unmarried and the widows" (verses 8-9) should be taken for granted here.

Paul's firm, even though not entirely unqualified, prohibition of divorce is probably directed to the same problem of asceticism in Corinth that had been his concern in the earlier paragraphs about marriage. There he had urged that conversion to Christianity does not require, or really even allow, a husband and a wife to abstain from sexual union. He does not condone celibate marriages. Now he is saying, in addition, that conversion to Christianity does not require divorce, either. This must have been another way some of the Corinthian ascetics had chosen to deny their sexuality. Paul believes this to be as equally unacceptable as celibate marriages. The marriage should be maintained in its full integrity. It is important to understand that Paul has not been asked to provide instructions for Christian couples whose marriages are in danger of falling apart because of a lack of "communication," or of mutual respect, or of common goals and values. At the outset, we established that marriage as such is not the subject of I Corinthians 7. Neither is divorce. The subject is sex, and more specifically whether marriage is any longer a legitimate status for one who belongs to Christ's body. Paul writes more as a "theologian" than as a "pastoral counselor" here, when he says that Christian marriages should not be dissolved. He is addressing an issue that has been raised for the Corinthians because of the particular ideology some of them have espoused.

There are several ways in which the parenthetical remark in verse 11 might be explained. Perhaps the Apostle knows of one or more specific instances of divorce that have already occurred in Corinth, and this provision is for those particular persons. Or, perhaps more likely, he is allowing in general for the possibility that some Christians may, despite his assurances, regard separation as the only way in Christ. If so, Paul's attitude toward them would be roughly analogous to the attitude he displays in the next chapter of this same letter. There the issue is whether Christians are free to eat meat that has been butchered in the worship of pagan gods. Paul himself clearly sides with those who have no compunctions of conscience in the matter. At the same time, however, he allows for those who believe that abstention from such meat is the only Christian way, and urges the others to show concern for them. (See, for example, I Cor. 8:9-13.) In chapter 7, where the issue is abstention from sex by the dissolution of Christian marriages, his own views are equally clear. But here again, we may have evidence (now in the parenthetical remark of verse 11) of his tolerant attitude toward those whose consciences will not allow them to continue in marriage.

Yet a third possibility is that Paul is thinking momentarily of Christians who may divorce for other reasons, reasons that he would consider warranted. This might explain his reference to the appropriateness of the couple's reconciliation. One must beware of reading too much into the word "reconciliation" here; but Paul's introduction of it into the discussion does suggest that he is not insensitive to the need for a genuinely caring relationship between persons if a marriage is to be fully authentic.

A final possibility is that the parenthesis has been intruded at a later time into the text of I Corinthians, either deliberately or accidentally. This could easily happen as the ancient scribes copied and recopied manuscripts that, not infrequently, contained marginal notations placed there by earlier readers. There is no evidence that such occurred in this instance, but it cannot be ruled out.

The topic of divorce is also present in verses 12-16. Here, however, the specific issue is different. The concern is about what course of action a Christian should follow when she or he converts to Christianity and the other partner in the marriage does not. (Whether a Christian should enter into a marriage with a non-Christian is not raised or answered. Paul has already dealt with the more fundamental question of whether the Christian should marry at all.) This matter is probably still related to the more general subject of sex in the Christian life. The earliest Christians had inherited from Judaism the belief that the sexual union between a man and a woman is a union of *persons,* of *whole beings,* not just a superficial physiological connection. Therefore, it is not entirely surprising to find the Corinthian ecstatics particularly distressed about the sexual union of a man or woman "in Christ" with an unbelieving spouse. Must not this union, at least, be broken off? Would not the continuation of a marriage where only one partner had been converted be a serious violation of Christ's body? Paul does not believe so, and his reasoning, which on the face of it seems obscure to us, rests finally on certain practical considerations.

For one thing, he argues, it may be that a Christian partner will eventually succeed in converting the non-Christian partner. "Wife, how do you know whether you will save your husband? Husband, how do you know whether you will save your wife?" (verse 16). One should not preclude this possibility by hasty separation. In this connection it is worth noting that Paul does not presume that the wife will automatically pledge herself to her husband's religion. The Greek moralist Plutarch, born about A.D. 46, reflects the usual view of Paul's contemporaries when he advises newlyweds that

> it is becoming for a wife to worship and to know only the gods that her husband believes in, and to shut the front door tight upon all queer rituals and outlandish superstitions. For with no god do stealthy and secret rites performed by a woman find any favor. ("Advice to Bride and Groom," 140.19)

For Paul, however, faith must have the character of a genuine decision, a free commitment of will, or else it is not really faith. Therefore, he does not seem to presume that a husband's conversion to Christianity will automatically mean the wife's espousal of the new faith, any more than he presumes that a husband's refusal to convert will preclude his wife's conversion.

In the second place, Paul reasons that these mixed marriages must be "holy" marriages, since the church does not in fact consider children born of one to be "non-Christian" in the same way the unbelieving partner is. Paul's argument can be laid out best in the form of a syllogism:

Major premise: Holy children are produced by holy marriages.

44

Minor premise: Mixed marriages produce holy children.
Conclusion: Mixed marriages are holy marriages.

Admittedly, the Apostle himself has not formulated his argument
this clearly, but this is the implicit logical structure of it. The minor
premise is quite apparent in the remark of verse 14*b,* addressed
to believers married to unbelievers, that "your children . . . are
holy." The major premise, left unexpressed, would have been
axiomatic, given Paul's belief that sexual union is an essential
part of marriage. And the conclusion is legitimately inferred from
verse 15*a,* where Paul says that the new life (holiness) brought to
the marriage by the Christian partner may effect new life in the
unconverted spouse. In effect, this conclusion becomes the
minor premise of a second syllogism. Thus:

Major premise: Holy marriages should be maintained. (See
verses 10,11.)
Minor premise: Mixed marriages are holy marriages.
Conclusion: Mixed marriages should be maintained.

Paul identifies one significant condition for the maintenance of
these mixed marriages. They must be marked by harmony and
concord, "for God has called us to peace" (verse 15*b*). Thus, if
the unbelieving partner is unwilling to continue the relationship,
the Christian partner should not force the issue (verse 15*a*).
Perhaps the Apostle has in mind cases where an unbelieving
spouse would make the partner's renunciation of his or her faith
a condition for continuing the marriage. Or he may be thinking
of the difficulties created where marriage partners are committed
to different priorities, goals, and values. Whichever the case, he
would appear to be unwilling to sanction the idea that marriage is
an end in and of itself that must be maintained at any cost. Here
Paul shows a sensitivity to the importance of the *quality* of a
marriage relationship for which he is seldom given credit. When,
practically, the relationship between a husband and wife is no

45

longer characterized by mutual respect, love, and faithfulness, then separation is permissible.

Conclusion

May the instructions about marriage and divorce in I Corinthians 7 still have meaning for modern Christians? The realities of Christian existence as Paul understood them in the first century were, in some major respects, different from the realities we face in the twentieth. Unlike Paul, we must reckon with a social and political order of indefinite duration. We are aware, sometimes painfully so, that "the form of this world" is constantly—and rapidly—changing, but we cannot share his view that its "passing" is imminent. Although the characteristics of "Corinthian" Christianity—its ecstatic experiences, its arrogant spirituality, its wavering between libertinism and asceticism—have appeared in one way or another throughout the history of the church, the forms they take in modern Christianity are significantly different from the conditions Paul saw in Roman Corinth. Nevertheless, if we keep these differences in mind, and do not expect all of our twentieth-century problems and questions to be solved for us, Paul's instructions here can still provide guidance in our day.

One more basic caution. We must remember that I Corinthians 7 is addressed to a specific dispute about sex in Corinth. It is not an essay on "the Christian family." If it seems, as laypersons have on occasion complained to me, that "Paul is preoccupied with the sexual part of marriage," that is because sex in marriage is the issue that the Corinthians had appealed to him. We shall be disappointed if we expect to find more than hints of the Apostle's views on other aspects of marriage and family life. He says nothing, for example, about the responsibilities of parenthood, or how these might figure into the question of maintaining or breaking up a marriage. So let us take what we find here, and not chastise Paul for what we do not find. What one does find here is, in fact, rather impressive.

1. *A consistent emphasis on the mutuality of the marriage relationship.* Paul regards the husband and wife as equal partners. They are to share decisions and responsibilities. They are to respect and care for each other. They are to remain faithful to each other. The Apostle emphasizes the importance of mutuality in connection with two areas where conflicts between persons are most apt to arise, religion and sex. We have already seen how, unlike his contemporary, the Greek moralist Plutarch, Paul presumes that a wife's religious commitments must be genuinely her own, not dictated by her husband's. And we have also noted Paul's emphasis on mutual sexual satisfaction. In this area, too, the contrasting attitude voiced by Plutarch helps us appreciate the distinctiveness of Paul's Christian teaching. The "true mistress of the household," writes Plutarch, is "not to avoid or to feel annoyed at [sexual advances] on the part of her husband if he begins them, [but] on the other hand [she is not] to take the initiative herself; for the [latter] course is meretricious and froward, the [former] disdainful and unamiable" ("Advice to Bride and Groom," 140.18). Paul's teaching on this matter also contrasts with the Jewish view of sex in marriage. The Apostle follows good rabbinic precedent when he teaches the maintenance of regular sexual relations within marriage. But in rabbinic teaching the responsibilities for this are placed on the husband exclusively. A rabbinic saying found in the Talmud (*Pes.* 72*b*) is typical: "A man is required to make his wife happy." According to the rabbinic view, a marriage must be clearly and entirely under the husband's direction.

At this point something should be said about the passages in Ephesians and Colossians that have been quoted so often in support of the idea that the wife's role in marriage is to serve her husband and to be subordinate to him in every way (Eph. 5:21-33; Col. 3:18-19). Don't these contradict the emphasis on mutuality that is so prominent in I Corinthians 7? As noted earlier, there are good reasons to think Paul did not write Ephesians or Colossians. Specifically, the passages in question are oriented to marriage and the family as ongoing social institutions. We have seen that Paul's own teaching was not. Even so, as careful studies of the admonitions in Ephesians and Colossians have shown, the importance of mutual respect and care between the parties of a marriage is still emphasized, and in this and other ways these passages differ fundamentally from the ideas about marriage and family that were widespread outside the Christian community. (See further below, pp. 89-91.)

2. *A concern for the character of the relationship between husband and wife.* Even though, because of the special issues in Corinth, this concern is not spelled out, it is pervasive. Paul had reminded the Thessalonians that a man should "take a wife for himself in holiness and honor, not in the passion of lust like heathen who do not know God" (I Thess. 4:4-5). In common with the Judaism out of which he came, the Apostle regards marriage as a part of the goodness of God's creation. Thus, in the apocryphal book of Tobit from the second century B.C., the creation story of Genesis 2 is invoked as offering the prototype of a true marriage. On the night of his wedding to Sarah, Tobias, Tobit's son, prays:

> Thou madest Adam, and Eve his wife to be his helper and support; and those two were the parents of the human race. This was thy word: "It is not good for the man to be alone; let us make him a helper like him." I now take this my beloved to wife, not out of lust but in true marriage. Grant that she and I may find mercy and grow old together. (8:6-7 NEB)

There is no reason to think that now, as Paul writes to the Corinthians, he is any less aware than usual of the importance of the quality of married life. He knows full well that exploitation (for example, sexual) of another person can occur as well within a marriage as apart from marriage. When he says that persons with strong sexual feelings should marry, he is certainly not reducing marriage to the status of a safety valve for pent-up lusts. That is what he sees it to be among the "heathen who do not know God." For those in Christ, the marriage relationship must be characterized by "holiness" and "honor." That is, each partner must affirm and support the existence and the personhood of the other. There must be faithfulness and love, harmony and concord. The peace to which God calls all his people must prevail.

3. *A recognition that individual cases may be different, and that different circumstances may require different actions.* It is remarkable how many varied patterns of action Paul allows for in this chapter. Some should remain single, others should marry. Some should maintain their marriages, others should probably separate. Some formerly married persons should remain unmarried; others may remarry. Some betrothals should proceed to marriage, some should not. And at one point Paul interrupts his instructions to say he is intending not to lay down *restraints,* but "to promote good order and to secure [the Christian's] undivided devotion to the Lord" (verse 35). Flexibility, then, is a prominent characteristic of the teaching here. The Apostle is keenly aware of the way circumstances may vary from case to case, and he takes account of this so far as it is possible for him to do so.

There are only a few points on which Paul seems to allow for *no* options, and because there is so much flexibility elsewhere, these are worth noting. He insists, of course, on monogamy. A husband should have but one wife, and a wife but one husband. Marriage to a second person after the death of a spouse is not seen as a violation of this, but it is not clear whether Paul would allow for remarriage to another person after divorce. Second, he allows no exception to the rule that sexual union should take place only where there is a marital relationship. Extramarital sex

49

is immoral. The question of *premarital* sex, as modern Christians are facing it, is not on Paul's agenda. We cannot even be sure that he would have understood the problem, since we know little about betrothal and marriage customs within the Pauline congregations. And in the third place, Paul allows for no variation from the rule that there shall be no permanent abstention from sex within marriage. Sexual union is both a legitimate and an important part of the relationship, as he sees it. He does not appeal to the responsibility for procreation to justify this. Given his view of the impending close of history he could not have shared that traditional Jewish concern. Instead, his conviction seems to be that the fulfillment of strong sexual feelings is good and proper even where procreation is not envisioned. He insists, however, that this sexual fulfillment is only meaningful where it takes place between two persons committed exclusively to each other and bound together in their mutual respect, care, and love.

For Further Reading

There is no shortage of books and articles on the topics discussed in this chapter. Unfortunately, many of them are highly biased and based on an uncritical analysis of the biblical materials. Responsible, basic information can be found in the various articles on "Marriage," "Divorce," "Kinship and Family," "Sex," and "Sexual Behavior" in *The Interpreter's Dictionary of the Bible,* 5 volumes (Nashville: Abingdon, 1962 and 1976), especially in the Supplementary Volume. Further basic bibliographical information is appended to each article.

The book by Evelyn and Frank Stagg, *Woman in the World of Jesus* (Philadelphia: Westminster Press, 1978) is helpful in several ways. The chapter on "The Domestic Code and Woman," which treats relevant materials in I Peter and the Pastoral Epistles as well as Ephesians and Colossians, is especially good, and a valuable supplement to the more restricted discussion above. I am in less accord with the interpretation of I Corinthians 7 in the chapter on Paul, chiefly because I think the peculiar situation Paul faced in Corinth has not been taken seriously enough. Nevertheless, this discussion, too, supplements mine in certain ways, and it is in agreement with mine in some basic ways. Separate chapters on woman in Judaism and in Greek and Roman society provide good general background, and there is a bibliography.

The quotation on page 33 above is taken from Kenneth J. Foreman's exposition of I Corinthians in *The Layman's Bible Commentary,* Vol. 21 (Richmond: John Knox Press, 1961), p. 85, and the quotation on page 35 is from David L. Dungan, *The Sayings of Jesus in the Churches of Paul* (Philadelphia: Fortress Press, 1971), p. 85. A detailed discussion of I Corinthians 7:10-11 in relation to the passages in the Synoptic Gospels constitutes about one-half of Dungan's book. It is here that one may find the argument that the exception-clause belongs to the earliest, not the latest, version of Jesus' saying.

The quotations from Plutarch's "Advice to Bride and Groom" are from Frank C. Babbitt's translation in The Loeb Classical Library, *Moralia,* Vol. II (Cambridge, Mass.: Harvard University Press, 1928). Plutarch's whole essay is worth reading for the light it sheds on non-Christian ideas about marriage in the first century A.D. A useful study of Jewish practice is Louis M. Epstein's *Sex Laws and Customs in Judaism* (New York: Ktav, 1967 [first published in 1948]).

Among the standard commentaries on I Corinthians, those by H. Conzelmann, trans. J. W. Leitch for the Hermeneia series (Philadelphia: Fortress Press, 1975), and C. K. Barrett in the Harper's New Testament Commentaries series (New York: Harper, 1968), are the most adequate. My views on Ephesians and Colossians are set forth in *The Interpreter's One-Volume Commentary on the Bible* (Nashville: Abingdon, 1971).

III

Homosexuality

When a group of representative laypersons and clergy in a major Protestant denomination were asked to indicate the sources that had contributed to their "present attitudes and opinions concerning homosexuality," *scripture* was named significantly more often than any other source as having contributed the most. The same poll disclosed that a high percentage of those questioned agreed that "homosexual activity is a sin." Their views, it would appear, are accurately mirrored in a letter written to the editor of a large metropolitan newspaper about the "sin" of homosexuality:

> I can much more easily respect and understand an atheist or agnostic accepting homosexuality than an individual who alleges to take the Bible seriously. Scripture is unequivocal on the subject, and to interpret it in any other way is to play fast and loose with God's word. (Dallas *Times Herald,* March 31, 1978)

As it happens, the scriptural texts that are most directly relevant to this question are found in Paul's letters. Because they have been so often invoked and so variously interpreted in the debates about the church and homosexuality, they deserve our careful consideration.

Several questions must be addressed in this chapter. First, what did Paul actually say about homosexuality? Second, what meaning does Paul's teaching on the subject have in our day? In order to answer these, two further questions will have to be considered. What were the realities of homosexual practice in Paul's day; that is, what empirical data were available to him? And, finally, what are the realities of homosexual practice in our day; what empirical data are available to us? Before turning to these questions, however, some preliminary remarks must be made about the status of the biblical evidence in general.

Finding the Biblical Texts

I once had an urgent telephone call from the host of a local television program. He was scheduled to interview a "gay rights" leader in a few days, and he wanted to confront him with the biblical injunctions against homosexuality. He could not find the passages, he confessed, and would I please help him?

That interviewer had already discovered something important, although he scarcely realized it: *homosexuality is not a prominent biblical concern.* The earliest ethical codes of the Hebrews make no mention of homosexual behavior. There is nothing about it in the Ten Commandments. The four Gospels record no saying of Jesus on the subject. The texts that are discussed in this connection are few and far between, and not even all of these are really pertinent. As we begin an investigation of the biblical teaching about homosexuality, then, we must keep our sense of proportion. We are not dealing with a fundamental biblical theme. We are not dealing with a major biblical concern. We have to *hunt* for relevant passages.

It must also be stressed that a Bible concordance is of only limited help in locating these passages. There were no words in Hebrew or in ancient Greek equivalent in meaning to our English words "homosexual" and "homosexuality." Even the English terms and the concepts behind them are of relatively modern origin. (The *Oxford English Dictionary* says of the noun only that it was in use before 1897.) The words do not appear anywhere in the King James Version of 1611. In fact, the first use of the term "homosexuals" in an English Bible did not come until 1946, with the publication of the Revised Standard Version of the New Testament. In that translation it represents two Greek words included in a list of "vices" in I Cor. 6:9, however in the second edition of the RSV New Testament (1971), and thus in the RSV Common Bible (1973), it is dropped in favor of the phrase "sexual perverts" (see below). Some other modern versions continue to employ it in this passage, either as the noun "homosexuals" (for example, *The Living Bible* and the New American Standard Version), or as an adjective ("homosexual perversion" in the New English Bible and "homosexual perverts" in Today's English Version).

Other recent translations, for example the Jerusalem Bible and the New American Bible, use the noun "sodomite" to refer to a male who engages in homosexual activity. This word has a much longer history of use in the English language than "homosexual," and, along with "sodomy," has become a technical term for a type (or types) of sexual activity prohibited by law. The King James Version uses "sodomite(s)" in Deuteronomy 23:17; I Kings 14:24; 15:12; 22:46; II Kings 23:7. Here, again, however, one must beware of placing too much confidence in an English concordance.

The English words "sodomy" and "sodomite" are formed from the name of the ancient city of Sodom. According to Genesis 19, two angels disguised as men came to Sodom and were offered hospitality in Lot's house. After dinner, and before Lot's guests had retired for the night, all the men of Sodom surrounded the house and shouted, "Where are the men who came to you tonight? Bring them out to us, that we may know them" (19:5). The Hebrew word "to know" can be used with reference to sexual relations, and it certainly is used so here, despite occasional claims to the contrary. Lot offers his virgin daughters instead (19:8). The men of Sodom decline the daughters, however, and press forward to do violence to Lot as well as to his guests. Their attack is repulsed only when the visitors cause them to be blinded (19:11). Thereupon Lot is advised to leave Sodom because, his visitors tell him, "The Lord is about to destroy the city" (19:14). Thus it was, that brimstone and fire rained down from heaven on Sodom and neighboring Gomorrah (19:24-25), so that the next morning only the smoking ruins could be seen (19:27-28).

Many recent writers, sponsors of what may be called a revisionist interpretation of the story of Sodom, have argued that homosexuality is not involved at all here. They insist that the men of Sodom were guilty only of inhospitality to the visiting strangers. In their view, the verb "to know" does not have a sexual meaning in this case, but only its usual meaning of getting acquainted, finding out who the strangers are and what they are about. This interpretation is not persuasive, however. For one thing, the context makes the sexual meaning of "to know" likely; certainly that is how Lot understands the demand when, in response, he offers his own daughters to the men who make it. Moreover, in Judges 19 there is a similar story of an Ephraimite who stops over in Gibeah for a night's lodging. He, too, is besieged by the men of the city, who cry out to his host that they want to "know" the stranger (Judges 19:22). Again the host offers to substitute his own virgin daughter, or else the visitor's concubine. The offer was declined, but when the concubine was put out to them anyway, "they knew her, and abused her all night until the morning" (Judges 19:25). Clearly, the objective of the men of Gibeah was sexual. Had the Ephraimite himself been attacked it would have been an act of homosexual rape. As it turned out, they abused his concubine instead. It is likely that this story in Judges has been influenced by the Genesis story of the men of Sodom. In each case the men of the city intended a homosexual assault on the visiting stranger. In this respect the revisionist interpretation must be corrected. The story is about sexual lust and violence—in the instance of Sodom, the unfulfilled lust of men directed against men.

We must recognize, however, that later biblical writers were not themselves preoccupied with this homosexual dimension of the old story. The reference to the "abominations" of Sodom in Ezekiel 16:47 probably has the (homo)sexual lust in view, but those abominations are described principally as having to do with "pride, surfeit of food, and prosperous ease," and with a refusal to "aid the poor and the needy" (Ezek. 16:48-50). In some other Jewish writings the crime is understood to have been not the desire of men to have sexual relations with men, but the desire of human beings to have sexual relations with angels, for that is who Lot's visitors really were. (See *The Testament of Naphtali* 3:4-5.) Echoes of this point of view are heard in Jude 6 and 7 and II Peter 2:4-8 in the New Testament. But elsewhere in the New Testament, as very often in the Old, it is the totality of the *destruction* of Sodom and not the particular nature of its crime for which the city is remembered. Thus, Sodom is a symbol for the reality of God's judgment, not a symbol for homosexuality—or even for sexual lust more generally. See, for example, Matthew 10:15 and the parallel in Luke 10:12, and Matthew 11:23-24. The one mention of Sodom in Paul's letters falls into this same category. It is, in fact, not even Paul's own reference, but is quoted by him from Isaiah 1:9. The scriptural text is used by Paul in order to assure his readers of the plight that befalls those against whom God has cause to direct his wrath (Rom. 9:29).

Two Jewish writers contemporary with Paul do refer to the homosexual aspect of the crime at Sodom. One of these is the Alexandrian philosopher Philo, who, in a vivid passage in his essay *On Abraham,* details the various excesses of the Sodomites including the practice of intercourse between males (XXVI.133-136). The other is the historian Josephus, a sometime confidant of Roman emperors. In his *Jewish*

56

Antiquities (I.200-201) he comments that "the Sodomites, on seeing these young men of remarkably fair appearance whom Lot had taken under his roof, were bent only on violence and outrage to their youthful beauty." Significantly, however, homosexual practice is only one of a number of charges Philo lists against them (his remarks will be discussed further below), and the main criticism Josephus has for the Sodomites is their pride, insolence, and refusal to respect the rights and needs of strangers in their midst (see especially *Jewish Antiquities* I.194-195, where, contrary to what some have claimed, Josephus does *not* use the term "sodomy" to mean homosexual intercourse; the term is not used at all.) It is really first of all in the Christian literature of the second century A.D. that Sodom becomes an unambiguous symbol of homosexuality, specifically of the sexual exploitation of young men by older men. Subsequently, the terms "sodomy" and "sodomite" came to be used as they are today in English.

It must be emphasized that the development of the sodomitic symbolism sketched above is not in evidence in the Bible itself. Although one may find the word "sodomite" used in some English versions, even recent ones like the second edition of the RSV New Testament (I Tim. 1:10), the Jerusalem Bible and the New American Bible, no Hebrew or Greek word formed on the name "Sodom" ever appears in the biblical manuscripts on which these versions are based.

In every instance in the King James Version where the term "sodomite" is used, the reference is to male prostitutes associated with places of worship. The practices of the ancient Canaanite and Babylonian fertility cults persisted in Palestine after the Hebrew settlement there, and their rites included the use of both male and female prostitutes. The potential, and in some cases actual, influence of these ancient practices was a persistent concern of the leaders of Israel. It is important to notice that our Old Testament texts attack the male prostitutes not because they engage in sexual relationships with other males; they, like the female prostitutes, are attacked because they serve alien gods. "Sodomite," therefore, is an improper translation; the one adopted in the RSV and other modern versions is much superior, "male cult prostitute." These passages are not about homosexuality, but about foreign idolatries. Thus, for example, King Asa is praised because "he put away the male cult prostitutes out of the land, and removed all the idols that his fathers had made" (I Kings 15:12).

Where, then, can we find the biblical texts worth considering in relation to the question about homosexuality?

The only Old Testament references that still require discussion are to be found in the so-called Holiness Code of Leviticus, chapters 17–26. Here we encounter the earliest specific legislation in Israel against homosexual practices (Lev. 18:22 and 20:13). These laws are part of Paul's heritage from Judaism, and they will be discussed in that connection below.

In the New Testament, apart from occasional references to Sodom (which do not mention the nature of the Sodomites' crime), we have three passages only. Two of these are Pauline—Romans 1:26-27 and I Corinthians 6:9. The third text is I Timothy 1:10. Not only is this the least helpful of the three New Testament passages, but it also stands in a writing that most scholars are unwilling to attribute to Paul himself. The first two passages are those which will have to claim our closest attention.

Homosexuality in Paul's World

Before we can evaluate Paul's remarks about homosexual practice or determine his intentions in the two relevant passages, we must understand something about the place of homosexuality in Greco-Roman society. We must also make ourselves aware of the attitudes toward it expressed in the moral teachings of Paul's contemporaries, Greco-Roman, rabbinic, and

Hellenistic Jewish. Only when we have some acquaintance with the phenomenon of homosexuality as Paul's world observed and analyzed it will be able to deal sensitively with the original meaning of the Pauline texts and with their significance for modern Christians.

Beginning in the sixth century B.C., homosexual love had a relatively prominent place in Greek social life. As several historians have noted, this coincided with the development of a commercial economy based on the institution of slavery and the use of money in business transactions. It coincided also with the increasingly subordinate role assigned to women in Greek society. Women had come to be valued only for their part in helping to ensure the continuation of the race. In this social climate homosexuality took the form primarily of *pederasty,* the love of an older man for a younger. The male youth was praised for his beauty, and the love of a man for a boy was extolled by philosophers, not least by Plato, as the purest form of love. On the island of Crete it was thought shameful for a boy not to have a lover, a custom that may have derived from ancient puberty rites. In Boeotia, it was reported, men and boys paired off into actual marriages.

Among the Greeks, it appears, pederasty played an important role in a youth's education. Moreover, when Plato described pederasty as among the noblest of all human relationships, his thought was not of a physical relationship but of a "higher" form of love uniting two persons—what we have come to call a Platonic relationship. More than likely these relationships were often physical as well, but it was not the physical as such that called forth the praise of the philosophers. Much the same may be said about the early-sixth-century poetess, Sappho. She presided over an intimate community of young women on the island of Lesbos and was famous, even in antiquity, for her love poems, many of them lyric odes to the beauties of her young proteges. The description of female homosexuality as "lesbian-

59

ism" derives from this community of women and young girls, even though Sappho herself was married and had a daughter.

When we come to the Roman period, and specifically to the world of the first century A.D. in which Paul lived, the situation is significantly different. Homosexuality is still openly practiced, especially among the upper classes, and its merits are still sometimes discussed in the philosophical literature. But increasingly, now, the moral philosophers of the day are questioning its merit, especially when they compare it with a heterosexual relationship in marriage. Increasingly, homosexual practices are associated with the grosser forms of self-indulgence. Several examples from literature essentially contemporary with Paul's life and ministry are worth citing. Taken together, these help to give us a picture of what Paul must have had in mind when he spoke of homosexual practices. They also indicate what some other thoughtful—and in each case non-Christian—writers were saying about such practices.

The distinguished philosopher, moralist, and statesman Seneca was named a Roman praetor in A.D. 49 and simultaneously appointed tutor to the young Nero. Nero's mother was at that time married to the Emperor Claudius, and upon Claudius' death five years later, Nero became his successor. Seneca thereupon became the new emperor's political adviser, and remained so until A.D. 62 when, disillusioned with Nero's policies, he retired from public life. Seneca's *Moral Epistles* were written during this period of retirement, and they reflect his concern about the lack of moral reason and responsibility in his society. Seneca deplores the way dissolute men of luxury exploit their slaves, and he offers one example that, for our present topic, is of special interest. At a banquet, Seneca complains, the slave who serves the wine

must dress like a woman and wrestle with his advancing years; he cannot get away from his boyhood; . . . he is kept beardless by having his hair smoothed away or plucked out by the roots, and he must remain awake throughout the night, dividing his time between his master's drunkenness and his lust. (*Moral Epistles* XLVII, "On Master and Slave," 7)

Seneca has here given us a picture of homosexual practice that springs from lust, is associated with idle luxury and moral debauchery, and that takes the form of a grotesque exploitation of another person, a male slave kept artificially youthful in appearance and forced into transvestitism. We are here far removed from the Greek ideal of pure love as it was hymned by Plato.

Plutarch, the Greek biographer, essayist, and moralist, was born about A.D. 46 and died about A.D. 120. His works also give us helpful information about the social environment in which Paul's ministry was conducted. Plutarch was well acquainted with Athens; he had traveled in Egypt, lectured in Rome, and for several decades served as a priest in the important city of Delphi. In his *Dialogue on Love* he has several young men debate whether handsome young Bacchon should marry the rich widow of Thespiae, a certain Ismenodora. Anthemion and Pisias, rivals for Bacchon's affections, have been asked to decide. Anthemion, joined by his friend Daphnaeus, is for the marriage, but Pisias, joined by his friend Protogenes, is against it.

Pisias argues, against the marriage, that decent women are incapable of either receiving or giving sexual pleasure (752B,C). Daphnaeus, on the other side, insists that "if union contrary to nature with males does not destroy or curtail a lover's tenderness, it stands to reason that the love between men and women, being normal and natural, will be conducive to friendship developing in due course from favour" (751C). The same speaker goes on to argue that "to consort with males . . . is a completely ill-favoured favour, indecent, an unlovely affront to Aphrodite [the Greek goddess of love and fertility]" (751D,E).

61

In an aside, Daphnaeus distinguishes between homosexual intercourse "without consent, in which case it involves violence and brigandage," and that which is "with consent," in which case "there is still weakness and effeminacy on the part of those who, contrary to nature, allow themselves in Plato's words 'to be covered and mounted like cattle.'"

In Plutarch's dialogue there is a concern for the sexual exploitation that homosexuality involves, even where there is consent. There is also the typically Stoic aversion to whatever is "contrary to nature." This second point plays an especially important role in the strong condemnation of homosexual practice found in the works of another first-century writer, Dio Chrysostom. He was born about A.D. 40 and died sometime after A.D. 112. Banished from Rome early in the reign of Domitian (A.D. 81–96), Dio wandered for many years through Greece, the Balkans, and Asia Minor, preaching the standard ideas and values of the Stoics and Cynics. Two particular features of homosexual practice as he knew it stand out in his writings.

First, like Seneca, Dio saw homosexuality as essentially exploitative. In one place (*Discourse* LXXVII/LXXVIII.36) he refers to dissolute males "who, though there are women in abundance, through wantonness and lawlessness wish to have females produced for them from males, and so they take boys and emasculate them. And thus a far worse and more unfortunate breed is created, weaker than the female and more effeminate." In another place (*Discourse* XXI.6-10) Dio provides a concrete, and famous, instance of just such a thing. In A.D. 67, after the death of his second wife, Poppaea Sabina, Nero had his male lover, Sporus, mutilated. Sporus was then renamed "Sabina," and publicly married to the Emperor.

Second, Dio understood homosexuality to be an expression of absolutely insatiable lust. In his so-called Euboean discourse (*Discourse* VII) he identifies brothel-keeping as one occupation that is legitimate for neither the rich nor the poor.

Brothel-keepers, he complains, "bring individuals together in union without love and intercourse without affection, and all for the sake of filthy lucre" (133). Like Daphnaeus in Plutarch's dialogue, Dio asserts that prostitution blasphemes the goddess Aphrodite, "whose name stands for the normal intercourse and union of the male and female" (135). Moreover, he argues, in cities where the young women are thus corrupted, the corruption of young men is likely to follow. He reasons that men will grow weary of satisfying their lust for women, especially when, for a fee, they have ready access to the town prostitutes. Then, he warns,

> the man whose appetite is insatiate in such things, when he finds there is no scarcity, no resistance, in this field, will have contempt for the easy conquest and scorn for a woman's love, as a thing too readily given . . . and will turn his assault against the male quarters, eager to befoul the youth who will very soon be magistrates and judges and generals, believing that in them he will find a pleasure difficult and hard to procure (151-152).

Such men, concludes Dio, are like people addicted to wine who, when they have finally lost their taste for it, must "create an artificial thirst by the stimulus of sweatings, salted foods, and condiments." In his view, then, lust and the violation of the natural order go closely together as the cause and the result of homosexual behavior.

Before concluding these observations about homosexual practice and attitudes toward it in the Greco-Roman world, some comments must be made about Jewish teaching on the subject. The earliest specific law against homosexuality in Israel occurs in Leviticus. In 20:13 it had been decreed: "If a man lies with a male as with a woman, both of them have committed an abomination; they shall be put to death, their blood is upon them." The same law is present in Leviticus 18:22, but without reference to the death penalty. The Holiness Code in which this law stands (Leviticus, chapters 17–26) had its origin in the sixth century B.C., either during or just after the Babylonian Exile of the Hebrew people. The purpose of this legislation, made plain early on in the Code, was to establish the distinctiveness of the Jewish cultus over against all foreign cults:

> You shall not do as they do in the land of Egypt, where you dwelt, and you shall not do as they do in the land of Canaan, to which I am bringing you. You shall not walk in their statutes. You shall do my ordinances and keep my statutes and walk in them. I am the Lord your God. (18:3-4)

The original purpose of this Holiness Code should be remembered when considering the specific prohibitions contained within it. These are numerous and detailed, and include strictures against various kinds of incestuous relationships (chapter 18), against idolatry (19:4), against cross-breeding cattle, sowing two kinds of seed in one field, or wearing two kinds of fabrics (19:19), as well as against theft, lying, and many kinds of social injustice. In all of these ways the people of Israel were required to maintain their identity and integrity as the people of the one true God. The prohibition of males lying with males, like many of the other laws in this code, sought to identify practices that had been, and ought always to remain, essentially foreign to Israel's life.

Among the Jews, in contrast to the Greco-Roman world as a whole, homosexual behavior was not common. The later rabbis regularly invoked the Levitical prohibitions of it and applied them to intercourse between females as well as to intercourse between males. The rabbis regarded homosexual behavior as a typical Gentile vice, and from a passage in Josephus one can get some idea of how widespread this suspicion was among the Jews. When Antony asked Herod to send his young brother-in-law, Aristobulus, to Rome, Herod decided that it "would not be safe" because Antony was surely set on using the handsome youth "for erotic purposes" (*Jewish Antiquities,*

XV.28-29). Josephus himself, in an eloquent defense of Jewish morality and culture, *Against Apion,* echoes the Levitical laws when he writes proudly about the Jews' abhorrence of intercourse between males and of their specifying the death penalty for those who engage in it (II.199).

A passage in which Philo describes the vicious behavior of the Sodomites has already been mentioned. The Alexandrian philosopher's embellishments of the biblical account provide further evidence of the revulsion felt toward homosexual behavior even by Jews who had in many ways fallen under the influence of Hellenistic culture. The men of Sodom, writes Philo, had been debauched by their wealth. Corrupted by their own opulence and satiety,

> they threw off from their necks the law of nature and applied themselves to deep drinking of strong liquor and dainty feeding and forbidden forms of intercourse. Not only in their mad lust for women did they violate the marriages of their neighbors, but also men mounted males without respect for the sex nature which the active partner shares with the passive. . . . Then, as little by little they accustomed those who were by nature men to submit to play the part of women, they saddled them with the formidable curse of a female disease. (*On Abraham* 135-136)

Here the traditional Jewish abhorrence of homosexuality has found expression in terms current among Gentile moralists like Seneca and Dio Chrysostom. Such behavior is said to contravene "the law of nature" and to spring from unbridled lust.

These representative descriptions of and comments about homosexual behavior in the first century A.D., all from thoughtful, contemporary observers and critics of the social scene, suggest three important points that must be borne in mind as the Pauline texts are studied.

First, not only the terms, but also the concepts "homosexual" and "homosexuality" were unknown in Paul's day. These terms, like the terms "heterosexual," "heterosexuality," "bisexual," and "bisexuality," presume an understanding of human sexuality that was possible only with the advent of modern psychological and sociological analysis. The ancient writers quoted above were operating without the vaguest conception of what we have learned to call "sexual orientation." Dio Chrysostom, for instance, presumed that the same lusts that drove men to engage female prostitutes could drive them eventually to seduce other men. Similarly, Philo wrote of the Sodomites' sexual intercourse with men as if it were one form of their "mad lust for women." Moreover, both writers presumed, with their contemporaries, that one could by force of will *control* these appetites and conform oneself to the sexual behavior dictated by reason or "the law of nature."

Second, then, the critics of homosexual behavior invariably associated it with insatiable lust and avarice. Seneca portrayed it as a rich man's sport, Dio Chrysostom as the ultimate sexual debauchery, and Philo, with reference to Sodom, as one of the vile consequences of wanton luxury and self-centeredness. By Paul's day the old Platonic ideal of the pure, disinterested love between a man and a boy was coming to ruin on the hard realities of Roman decadence. One of the speakers in Plutarch's dialogue could acknowledge the possibility of genuine homosexual love, but even he saw a need to repeat Plato's warning about homosexual seduction; and his real point was that a man's love for a woman is potentially finer than one's love for another man.

Finally, the writers of this period who were concerned about homosexual behavior seemed convinced that it necessarily involved one person's exploitation of another. Stoicism, especially, maintained that one's life must be conducted in accord with the immutable law of nature and in ways appropriate to the created order. The influence of this popular philosophical movement was widespread, and is detectable not only in several of the writers quoted above but also, as we shall see, in the teaching of Paul. The physiological complementarity of male and female and the obvious necessity of heterosexual intercourse for the purposes of procreation would have seemed to many adequate proof that intercourse between persons of the same sex was "unnatural," a violation of "the law of nature." Thus, Plutarch's Daphnaeus admitted, even when both parties consent to homosexual intercourse, that the passive one is bound to be violated. He becomes what he is not—"weak" and "effeminate," and his weakness and effeminacy is more demeaning than that of a woman because it does not belong to the role nature has assigned him. On this view, if there is exploitation of one person by another even where there is consent, how much more where there is none? One thinks of the Sodomites' attempted rape of Lot's visitors, of the actions of a debauched master toward his slaves, or of lustful men toward helpless youth. (The point had not been lost on Philo, who, in the passage quoted above, mentions "the sex nature which the active partner shares with the passive.") To discerning ethical teachers in the Greco-Roman world it seemed just as obvious that homosexual practices were necessarily exploitative as that they were inevitably born of insatiable lust.

The Pauline Texts

The preceding section sought to indicate the ways in which certain writers contemporary with Paul perceived and criticized homosexual behavior. When we turn now to Paul's remarks about such conduct, it becomes apparent that he perceived it in essentially the same way. The picture we have obtained, notably from Seneca and Dio Chrysostom, of homosexual practices in Greco-Roman society, must closely approximate the picture Paul would have had in his mind as he, too, condemned such behavior. But Paul's ethical teachings, one must remember, are integrally related to his fundamental theological convictions, the most definitive of which were not shared by the writers we have considered so far. Therefore, in our analysis of the two relevant Pauline texts we shall need to be aware not only of the social context they presume, but also of the literary-theological contexts within which they stand. The reference in I Corinthians 6:9 is the briefer, more problematic, and overall less informative of the two. It will be well to start with this one, if for no other reason than that it has chronological precedence over the longer and more substantial remarks on the subject in Romans 1:26-27.

1. I Corinthians 6:9

In several recent English versions a reference to homosexuals appears in this verse. Thus, the first edition of the RSV lists "homosexuals" among those excluded from God's kingdom, and so does *The Living Bible.* The New English Bible uses "homosexual perverts," and the New American Bible has "sodomites." The second edition of the RSV New Testament (incorporated into the RSV Common Bible) broadens the concept with a reference to "sexual perverts," with which one may compare the rendering of the New International Bible, "the sexually immoral."

This picture becomes still more confused when one realizes that all the translations cited are using *one* word or phrase to render *two* distinct nouns in Paul's original Greek. Some other translations do try to reflect Paul's use of two different words, but here again the translations are quite varied. The King James Version had rendered them as "effeminate" and "abusers of themselves with mankind" respectively. The American Standard Version changed "mankind" to "men," and recently the New American Standard Version, while retaining the word "effeminate," has translated the second word as "homosexuals." James Moffatt's translation had used the words "catamites" and "sodomites," and these have been more recently revived in the Jerusalem Bible. Goodspeed, on the other hand, had interpreted them as references to those who are "sensual" and "given to unnatural vice," and in the version of J. B. Phillips one reads of the "effeminate" and the "pervert."

The two Greek words in question are *malakoi* and *arsenokoitai*. The root meaning of the first term is "soft" or "weak," and by extension, "effeminate," as in some translations of I Corinthians 6:9. Many scholars believe there is adequate evidence from its occurrence in ancient texts to conclude that it could be used more specifically to refer to the passive partner in male homosexual intercourse. That Paul is using it this way here seems likely, because it stands in a list where several other terms referring to sexual immorality also appear, for example "fornicators" (RSV renders this term too broadly, as "the immoral") and "adulterers." The second disputed term is compounded of the word for "male" or "masculine" and a word that refers to "ones who go to bed." In this case, most scholars conclude, the active partner in male homosexual intercourse is in mind.

The translation of the two words common to Moffatt's version and the Jerusalem Bible is based on the conclusions just outlined. The English word "catamite" refers to the male homosexual who plays the female role in intercourse, and the word "sodomite," as it has come to be used, refers to the active partner in such a relationship. A recent study by John Boswell questions the adequacy of the evidence on which these translations are based, however, and Boswell himself would render the words in question as "the dissolute" and "male prostitutes." If he is correct, I Corinthians 6:9 would have no importance for our investigation of Paul's ideas about homosexual practice. But since Boswell's arguments will not be persuasive to everyone, it is well to consider what this text does mean, if indeed it is relevant at all. Since no English version is fully satisfactory, I offer here my own translation.

> Don't you know that unrighteous persons will not get into God's kingdom? Don't deceive yourselves: neither the sexually immoral, nor idolators, nor adulterers, nor men who assume the female role in sex, nor men who have sex with them, nor thieves, nor money-grabbers, nor drunkards, nor slanderers, nor swindlers will get into God's kingdom. Some of you were like that; however, you have been cleansed, set apart for God's service, affirmed as righteous, in the name of the Lord Jesus Christ and in the Spirit of our God. (I Cor. 6:9-11)

In chapters 5 and 6 of I Corinthians, Paul is discussing various problems of sexual immorality. Beginning in chapter 7, as we have seen (above, chapter 2), he will deal with some questions (including some about sex) that had been put to him in a letter from Corinth. Here, however, he is responding, first of all, to some troubling news received by means of an oral report, perhaps from the bearer of the letter. He has learned that a member of the Corinthian congregation has taken up living with his stepmother, presumably now widowed (5:1). Paul directs that the man should be put out of their church because of his aberrant behavior (5:2-5). One gathers that the Corinthian Christians had not, themselves, been very worried about the matter. Paul is astonished at their smug complacency ("And you are arrogant!" 5:2) and he criticizes their spiritual pride (5:6-8).

This specific case of sexual immorality in Corinth prompts Paul, in 5:9-13, to clarify something he had said in an earlier letter (now lost). He had warned the Corinthians not to associate with persons guilty of sexual (and other) immoralities (5:9). Evidently the Corinthians had taken this to mean (or at least Paul thought they had taken it to mean) that they were to dissociate themselves from society at large. Not at all, says Paul! That is quite impossible (5:10). What he actually meant was that they should break off fellowship with other *Christians* who, like this fellow who is living with his stepmother, are guilty of serious immorality (5:11-13).

Paul's instruction to the Corinthians about disciplining errant members of their congregation moves him, in 6:1-11, to comment on the impropriety of Christians' taking their disputes to secular judicatories for settlement. Of course, it is a shame that any such disputes even arise within the church (6:7-8), but if they do, they should also be heard and settled there, not before "unbelievers" (6:6). Implicit in the argument of these verses is the Apostle's conviction that Christians do not belong, ultimately, to this world. Although they are for the present in this world (see 5:10), they are not "of" it. The world is not to judge them; indeed, because they are God's people the world is in a sense judged by them (6:2). Those who belong to the world are called "unbelievers" (6:6) and, later, "unrighteous persons" (6:9); Christians, on the other hand, are called "saints," people set apart for the service of God (6:1, 2). The question, "Don't you know that unrighteous persons will not get into God's kingdom?" (6:9a), simply emphasizes the distinction that had been implicit in the preceding discussion. On the one hand are the "saints" who belong to God's kingdom even while they are in this world; on the other hand are the "unbelievers" or "unrighteous" people who are not only in this world but belong to it, insofar as they submit to its claims and not to God's.

In 6:9b-10, to make his point yet more concrete, Paul offers a list of unrighteous types, examples of those who belong to this world rather than to God's kingdom. He uses similar lists in I Corinthians 5:10-11, Galatians 5:19-21, and Romans 1:29-31. Catalogs of vices are present elsewhere in the New Testament as well. The author of the so-called Pastoral Epistles, who wrote some years after Paul's death but under his name, incorporates such lists in several passages. The one in I Timothy 1:9-10 includes the second of the two disputed words in I Corinthians 6:9, and in I Timothy the RSV has translated it "sodomites." In

71

this list, as in Paul's own, it is one of a miscellaneous handful of vices chosen to identify actions displeasing to God.

No two New Testament vice lists are identical. Moreover, none is offered as a definitive formulation of all, or even of the chief evils Christians should avoid. When Paul closes the list in Galatians with the phrase "and the like" (5:21), it is clear that he intends such lists to be only exemplary. They only illustrate the kind and range of vices that he deems incompatible with the ways in Christ he teaches in all his churches. These catalogs have been assembled more or less at random. For the most part they contain the kinds of vices that Jews identified with pagan behavior, and similar catalogs are present in the moral literature of Hellenistic Judaism. Paul is probably thinking of the Gentile background of some (perhaps the majority) of the Christians in Corinth when he reminds them, "Some of you were like that" (6:11a). However, their baptism into Christ has now marked them as persons gifted with God's righteousness and God's Spirit, and set apart for his service.

The words Paul uses in this catalog for homosexual behavior (assuming he *is* using them with that reference) suggest that the picture in his mind is approximately that which one gets of the practice from the contemporary authors cited above. The one partner has violated the male role that by nature is his; and, by taking advantage of this, the other partner has also violated his proper role. Such conduct Paul regards as one of the forms of unrighteousness by which "unbelievers" are distinguished from "saints." Since he has just been writing about a specific case of sexual misbehavior, the Apostle's vice list here tends to be weighted slightly toward sexual offenses. Otherwise, however, the items seem to have been chosen at random and listed as they came to mind. Neither here nor elsewhere are such examples of wickedness identified as "sins." In fact, whenever the plural form, "sins," does appear in Paul's letters, it is either a quotation from scripture (once) or in a more or less set formula Paul has taken over from church traditions (four times). The Apostle himself thinks of sin (singular) both as a power that drives a wedge between God and his people and as the condition of alienation from God that results. The various kinds of vice and wickedness he lists here and elsewhere are presented as symptomatic of sin, not as its roots and essence. This important point becomes especially clear when we analyze the second passage and its context.

2. Romans 1:26-27

As noted above, one cannot be absolutely certain that the two key words in I Corinthians 6:9 are meant as references to male homosexual behavior. No such qualification needs to be made as we come now to the passage in Romans. There is still no *discussion* of such behavior, but the passage is more informative than the catalog of vices in I Corinthians. And here, for the first and only time in the whole Bible, one encounters the condemnation of female homosexuality as well as of male. Again with special reference to the immorality of pagan Gentiles, Paul writes: "Their women exchanged natural relations for unnatural, and the men likewise gave up natural relations with women and were consumed with passion for one another, men committing shameless acts with men and receiving in their own persons the due penalty for their error."

One is struck immediately by the similarities between this condemnation of homosexual behavior and that of Paul's non-Christian contemporaries. Like them Paul supposes that homosexual behavior is something *freely chosen* by an individual; in Greek as in English the verbs "exchanged" and "gave up" imply a conscious decision to act in one way rather than another. Like them Paul associates this choice with *insatiable lust;* the men, he says, were "consumed with passion" for other men. And like them, Paul regards such activity as *a violation of the created order;* "natural" heterosexual relations

73

were abandoned in favor of those which were "against nature" (RSV: "unnatural"). These similarities make it reasonable to suppose that the picture of homosexual practice Paul had in his mind corresponded closely to the depiction of it we have seen in the works of Seneca, Dio Chrysostom, and Philo.

The text in Romans, no less than the one in I Corinthians, needs to be appraised in the light of its literary and theological context in the letter of which it is a part. Romans, however, is not addressed to a congregation with which Paul is very well acquainted. He had not founded the church there, as he had the one in Corinth, and he had not even visited there. So far as we know, the Roman Christians had never written him, and it is debated whether any of the ethical teachings of Romans have specific "Roman problems" in mind.

The verses with which we are concerned here stand in a long discussion that begins at Romans 1:18 and continues through Romans 3:20. The best summary of this section of the letter is supplied by Paul himself as he moves into a new phase of his argument (3:22b-23): "For there is no distinction; since all have sinned and fall short of the glory of God. . . ." When he says "all," the Apostle means that Jews no less than Gentiles stand in need of God's gracious gift of justification. How justification comes—"by faith"—and what justification means are important themes from Romans 3:21 through chapter 8. In these chapters we are at the very heart of Paul's gospel. To this the preceding section, 1:18–3:20, provides an important introduction.

Put briefly, Romans 1:18–3:20 stresses the need of all people for the saving grace of God. In 1:18-32 the Apostle is denouncing the wickedness of the Gentiles in terms and with arguments that were the stock-in-trade of much Hellenistic Jewish teaching. Paul is heir to this, and commentators have long recognized the correspondence between his condemnation of the Gentiles here in Romans and that which appears in the apocryphal Wisdom of Solomon, written in Greek in the preceding century, probably by an Alexandrian Jew. In Wisdom 13:1-9, for example, the author argued that "all men who were ignorant of God were foolish by nature," unable to know God "from the good things that are seen," that is, from his creation (13:1). "For from the greatness and beauty of created things comes a corresponding perception of their Creator" (13:5). This writer is briefly tempted to admire the Gentiles, searching for God (13:6-7), but he finally has to conclude that "not even they are to be excused; for if they had the power to know so much that they could investigate the world, how did they fail to find sooner the Lord of these things?" (13:8-9). It was of course profoundly ironic that the Gentiles had failed to acknowledge the Lord and Creator of the very world that they seemed to understand so well in so many ways. But it was more than ironic; here it is regarded as the essence of their depravity. They mistook the stars of heaven for gods (13:2) and prayed to wooden figures they themselves had carved and painted (13:13-19). This is the ultimate folly, to be caught up with one's own devices and thereby alienated from one's own Creator.

The same interplay of ideas is present in Romans 1:18-32. Here again it is asserted that the world itself is testimony to the existence and sovereignty of God: "Ever since the creation of the world his invisible nature, namely, his eternal power and deity, has been clearly perceived in the things that have been made" (1:20a). Here again the Gentiles are given some credit: they do have a certain knowledge of God, Paul admits (1:21). Here again the conclusion follows that the Gentiles are all the more "without excuse" (1:20b) for their failure to recognize their sovereign Lord: "they did not honor him as God or give thanks to him" (1:21). And here again Gentile religions are denounced as foolish idolatries: "they became futile in their thinking and their senseless minds were darkened. Claiming to be wise, they became fools, and exchanged the glory of the immortal God for images resembling mortal man or birds or

75

animals or reptiles" (1:21, 22-23). Paul understands the old lesson very well: the grossest depravity of which human beings are capable is "[to exchange] the truth about God for a lie and [to worship and serve] the creature rather than the Creator" (1:25). The word "sin" does not happen to occur in Romans 1:18-32, but the taproot of sin is being described nonetheless. It is the refusal to acknowledge the true source and meaning of one's existence, and therefore the failure to acknowledge the grace and the claim under which one's whole life stands.

The closing paragraphs of Romans 1 have not yet been analyzed, and because Paul's remarks about homosexual conduct occur in them, this phase of the argument needs to be given our particularly close attention. It is opened in verse 24 with the statement that God "gave up" the Gentiles "to impurity." This is restated in verse 26a as his having given them up "to dishonorable passions." Then in verse 28 it is restated again, now in such a way as to connect this last phase of the argument with the earlier phases: "And since [the Gentiles] did not see fit to acknowledge God, God gave them up to a base mind and to improper conduct."

Here Paul is still under the influence of the traditions of Hellenistic Judaism, and the Wisdom of Solomon once more helps us grasp his meaning. In Wisdom 11:16 it is claimed that the Gentiles learned "that one is punished by the very things by which he sins." Since they had engaged in the idolatrous worship of "irrational serpents and worthless animals" (11:15; compare Rom. 1:23), their punishment came in the form of savage beasts like ravenous bears and lions (11:17-20). The point is not, however, that their wickedness automatically generated its own punishment. The punishment was *sent* upon them by God (11:16), even though in a form appropriate to the root idolatry. Similarly in Wisdom 12:17—the Gentiles first recognized the true God when they saw his hand in the punishment visited upon them by the very creatures that they had mistakenly worshiped. Paul, too, understands God to be the agent of punishment. He is the one who "gives up" the Gentiles to the appropriate consequences of their idolatries. It is thus "the wrath *of God*" that is "*revealed from heaven* against all ungodliness and wickedness of men" (Rom. 1:18).

In these closing paragraphs Paul is also being influenced by the traditional connection made in Hellenistic Judaism between idolatry and sexual immorality. The Wisdom of Solomon affords us an example.

> For the idea of making idols was
> the beginning of fornication
> and the invention of them was the
> corruption of life. (14:12)

Specific forms of immorality to which the Gentiles have submitted are cataloged in Wisdom 14:25-26: "All is in chaos—bloody murder, theft and fraud, corruption, treachery, riot, perjury, honest men driven to distraction; ingratitude, moral corruption, sexual perversion, breakdown of marriage, adultery, debauchery" (NEB). At the close of this listing it is reiterated that "the worship of idols, whose names it is wrong even to mention, is the beginning, cause, and end of every evil" (14:27 NEB). It is not surprising, then, to find Paul including sexual immoralities among those vices to which the pagans have been led by their own idolatry: lustful impurity and the degradation of their bodies (1:24), and "dishonorable passions" as evidenced by homosexual intercourse (1:26-27). In this connection he too can speak of the Gentiles having received "the due penalty for their error" (1:27).

The pattern of thought in Romans 1:18-32 should now be clear. It is a denunciation of the Gentiles formulated in accord with traditional Jewish reasoning. Although God's sovereign power was evident to the Gentiles in the created order, they chose to worship gods of their own making. They are therefore without excuse for their refusal to acknowledge their true

Creator and Lord. This is their sin, their attempt to exist apart from God. In consequence, God has now been "revealed" to them through his wrath (see Rom. 1:18), and the vices typical of Gentile society are the specific evidences of this. They are the penalties appropriate to the idolatries that have been committed.

Homosexual intercourse is mentioned as one of these typically Gentile practices (1:26*b*-27). It is regarded not as one of the "sins" of the Gentiles, but as one of the *consequences* of their root sin of refusing to let the one true God be *their* God. There is nothing in Paul's description of homosexual conduct, if we abstract it from the context in Romans 1:18-32, which could not have been written by Paul's non-Christian contemporaries, like Plutarch and Dio Chrysostom. And even granting the context, a Hellenistic Jew like Philo could just as well have written it. The particular function Romans 1:18-32 has in the whole of Romans 1–8, is another matter, however. Paul's condemnation of the Gentiles is only preludial to Romans 2:1–3:20, where he argues that also the Jews are sinners before God. Because they presume that they are justified by doing what the law requires (see, for example, 3:20), they too are guilty of trying to live on the basis of their own devices. So Paul can conclude (and he quotes scripture to prove it) that all peoples, "both Jews and Greeks, are under the power of sin" (3:9, followed by citations from the Psalms in verses 10-18). This is why God had acted in Christ to reconcile his people to himself, and this is the very gospel for which Paul had been made an apostle. The redemptive grace of God in Christ is the one great theme of all of Paul's letters and the fundamental theological basis of all of his ethical teaching.

Conclusion

In common with many "secular" moralists of his time and in accord with the teachings of the rabbis and of Hellenistic

Judaism, Paul condemns homosexual practices. However, he is not preoccupied with this matter (we have at most only two relevant texts in his letters) and there is no evidence that he ever had to deal with a specific case of homosexual conduct. His references to it are brief and formulated under the influence of traditional ideas about its causes and characteristics. In Romans, the most important text, his remarks do not even occur within a specific section of ethical teaching. They are a relatively incidental part of his argument that all people are sinners who stand in need of salvation. In the light of all of this, what shall we do with these texts today?

1. *Since Paul offered no direct teaching to his own churches on the subject of homosexual conduct, his letters certainly cannot yield any specific answers to the questions being faced in the modern church.* Shall practicing homosexuals be admitted to church membership? Shall they be accorded responsibilities within a congregation? Shall they be commissioned to the church's ministry? The Apostle never asks or answers these questions. He assumes that homosexual conduct is symptomatic of an individual's fundamental refusal to acknowledge God, so it is doubtful that such questions could ever have occurred to him. On these points there are no proof texts available one way or the other. It is mistaken to invoke Paul's name in support of any specific position on these matters.

2. *Paul, in common with the traditions by which he was influenced and in accord with the wisdom of his day, saw the wickedness of homosexual practice to inhere in its lust and its perversion of the natural order.* He, like many of his contemporaries, would have regarded such behavior as a matter of deliberate choice born of an insatiable sexual appetite. The moral legacy Paul had received from Hellenistic Judaism certainly left no doubt in his mind that it was a specifically Gentile vice and one of the numerous signs of pagan idolatry. In Romans 1 we have seen homosexual intercourse named as one of the dreadful conse-

79

quences of the Gentiles' refusal to receive the world as it was created and their own lives within it as gifts from God.

But what Paul accepted as a matter of course about homosexual behavior, we can no longer take for granted. The modern behavioral sciences are still baffled by many aspects of this phenomenon; yet there is broad agreement on a number of points. To begin with, one must now acknowledge that homosexuality is an exceedingly complex phenomenon. The description and analysis of it offered by ancient writers are as outdated as their descriptions of the bodily organs. The present scientific consensus is that homosexuality has multiple causes. Important psychological and social factors, and perhaps even some biological conditions, play a role in the formation of a person's "gender identity." Moreover, the forms and evidences of homosexuality are now understood to be many and varied. Modern students of the subject are reluctant to speak of homosexuality and heterosexuality as mutually exclusive categories. They much prefer to speak of homosexual and heterosexual *aspects* in the sexual orientation of a given individual. They refer to "latent" and "active' homosexuality, and allow that the latter can manifest itself in different ways, some of them more and some of them less socially acceptable. It is also clear that homosexual behavior does not necessarily involve the sexual exploitation of another person, and that it does not necessarily take the bizarre forms that were so evident in Paul's time.

If Paul had said somewhere that all mushrooms are "naturally poisonous," therefore those who eat mushrooms or cause others to eat them will not get into God's kingdom, we should think it important to reconsider his verdict in the light of our present-day knowledge. When in I Corinthians 11:14-15 he actually does say that it is unnatural for men to wear long hair and for women to wear their hair short, we find the judgment eccentric (the only "natural" thing is to let one's hair grow as long as it will!). Of course, human sexuality is an infinitely more complex phenomenon, indeed, far more complex than Paul and his contemporaries could have realized. Precisely for this reason, the Apostle's judgments in the matter require careful interpretation and evaluation if they are to be meaningful in the light of our present knowledge.

It would be unfair to charge Paul with naïvete or ignorance in the matter of homosexuality. Such evidence as we have suggests he was as informed as anyone could have been in his day. Indeed, *we* should be the naïve ones were we to ignore the data available to us in our own day, supposing that Paul's teaching alone is sufficient to answer our questions about right and wrong in this difficult matter.

3. *Paul's fundamental concerns about homosexual practice (as he understood it) are as valid in the twentieth century as they were in the first.* When Paul referred to homosexual behavior he was illustrating the wretchedness of the human condition where there has been no acknowledgment that life is God's gift and that one's existence stands always under God's claim. To Paul it represented a rebellion against the Creator and his creation, a surrender to one's own lusts, the debasement of one's own true identity and the exploitation of another's. It is no longer possible to share Paul's belief that homosexual conduct always and necessarily involves all these things. But it can be said with certainty that whenever a homosexual *or* heterosexual relationship does involve one or more of these, it stands under the judgment of scripture.

4. *Paul's remarks about homosexual behavior must not be isolated from the wider theological context in which they stand.* One must remember the function of Romans 1:18-32 in the letter as a whole. Paul repeats the standard Jewish accusations against the Gentiles in order to be able to say, respecting the Jews, "they are no better," and to emphasize that all stand in need of God's grace (2:1–3:20).

81

One must also remember that homosexual practice is mentioned in this context as just one of numerous vices that are symptomatic of sin. For Paul neither homosexual practice nor heterosexual promiscuity nor any other specific vice is identified as such with "sin." In his view the fundamental sin from which all particular evils derive is idolatry, worshiping what is created rather than the Creator, be that a wooden idol, an ideology, a religious system, or some particular moral code.

And finally, one must remember that 1:18–3:20 is itself prefatory to the good news about the reality of God's grace, which is expounded in the rest of Romans. Romans 5:6-11 is one classic summary of Paul's gospel: While we were still "weak," still "sinners," and still "enemies" of God, he reconciled us to himself through the love revealed and made real for us in Christ's death.

For Further Reading

D. S. Bailey's discussion of the biblical materials in his book *Homosexuality and the Western Christian Tradition* (London: Longmans, Green, 1955) has influenced much of the subsequent literature, though biblical scholars and others have challenged many of his conclusions. A more recent and more comprehensive examination of the biblical texts is Tom Horner's *Jonathan Loved David: Homosexuality in Bible Times* (Philadelphia: Westminster Press, 1978). Horner corrects Bailey in a number of important ways. It is unfortunate, however, that Horner feels constrained to argue for at least the possibility of homosexual relationships between Jonathan and David and Ruth and Naomi, respectively, and to hint at the homosexual characteristics of Jesus and Paul. Our sources simply do not provide the data to support such ideas. Horner's treatment of the Old Testament passages is, on the whole, better than his treatment of the Pauline texts.

John Boswell's book *Ganymede in Exile: Medieval Christianity, Homosexuality, and Intolerance* (New Haven: Yale University Press) had not been published and was not available to me when the present chapter was written. My knowledge of Boswell's thesis comes chiefly from Byron E. Shafer's paper, "The Church and Homosexuality," published in 1978 by the General Assembly of the United Presbyterian Church in the United States of America as a part of the report of its Advisory Council on Church and Society. Shafer himself provides one of the most balanced treatments of the biblical passages I have seen. His analysis of the findings of the modern empirical sciences is also useful, and there is a lengthy bibliography. Much more accessible to most readers will be Marvin Pope's article "Homosexuality" in *The Interpreter's Dictionary of the Bible,* Vol. 5, which also has a good bibliography.

In citing and quoting from non-Christian contemporaries of Paul, I have relied on The Loeb Classical Library as follows: Josephus, *Jewish Antiquities,* Book I trans. H. St. J. Thackeray (1930), Book XV trans. Ralph Marcus and Allen Wikgren (1963), and *Against Apion,* trans. H. St. J. Thackeray (1926); Philo, *On Abraham,* trans. F. H. Colson (1935); Seneca, *Moral Epistles,* XLVII trans. R. M. Gummere (1917); Plutarch, *Dialogue on Love,* trans W. C. Helmbold in Vol. IX of the *Moralia* (1961); Dio Chrysostom, *Discourse* VII trans. J. W. Cohoon (1932) and *Discourse* LXXVII/LXXVIII, trans. H. Lamar Crosby (1951).

The most important commentaries on Romans are those by Ernst Käsemann (Grand Rapids: Eerdmans, 1979) and C. E. B. Cranfield, *The Epistle to the Romans: Introduction and Commentary on Romans I-VIII,* 6th edition, entirely rewritten, in The International Critical Commentary (Edinburgh: T. & T. Clark, 1975). Commentaries on I Corinthians are noted at the end of chapter 3.

IV

Women in the Church

Our examination of Paul's references to marriage (chapter 2) disclosed that he regards the man and woman as fully equal partners and mutually responsible for the quality of the relationship. It is difficult to find real parallels to this emphasis in the ethical writings of Paul's contemporaries, either Jewish or non-Jewish. Now in this present chapter we must ask whether the Apostle holds any corresponding view about the equality of men and women within the life and ministry of the church.

In many Protestant denominations and in Roman Catholicism, the role of women within the church continues to be debated. The appropriateness of ordaining women has been bitterly contested, and the decision to do so in one major denomination led some local congregations to sever their ties with the national body. Even in denominations where the ordination of women has not been seriously questioned on doctrinal grounds, women clergy have often found the opportunities for ministry more limited for them than for their male counterparts. On this subject, as on the others we are surveying, Pauline texts have frequently been invoked by one side or the other, but probably more often by those who argue that women should *not* be accorded equal status in the church's ministry. The following two examples will illustrate the point.

An urban church in the Southwest, which belongs to a denomination in which the local congregations decide who shall be ordained, was proposing to ordain a woman into the ministry. Just before the final vote, one of its members arose to argue that this was not a proper role for a woman to have. He based his case primarily on the teaching of Paul. Appealing, for example, to the eleventh chapter of I Corinthians, he declared that there "Paul had set up roles for the kingdom of God," because Paul described God as the head of Christ, Christ as the head of man, and a man as the head of a woman. "These roles," he went on,

> were not culturally conditioned, but were begun with Adam and Eve. The roles for men and women are not the same and it is no disgrace or shame to either sex that their roles are different. The church structure is set up by God in line with the family structure. As Christ is head over the church and as the husband is head over the family, so men are to be the authorities in the body of believers.

He cited several other texts as well, including I Corinthians 14:34 ("the women should keep silence in the churches") and I Timothy 2:12 ("I permit no woman to teach or to have authority over men").

A more extreme example is that of a Protestant minister in the lower Midwest who conducted a question-and-answer column in a local newspaper. In response to a reader's question, he argued on the basis of I Timothy 2:11-12 that women are to have no major leadership roles in the church as a whole, thus no part in preaching, teaching, (solo) music, or prayer when men are present! When women assume such roles, he concluded, "they violate the positive command of God through Paul."

Both of these examples reflect the sacred-cow view of Paul's ethical teaching which was criticized in chapter 1. And they both illustrate how Paul's teaching on practical matters can be grossly distorted if one does not take account of *all* the evidence available and interpret it within the total context of Paul's world, of his gospel, and of his ministry.

The Problem of Sources

Before we can proceed very far with the topic before us, we must make some decisions about sources. There has been occasion earlier to note that Ephesians, Colossians, and the Pastoral Epistles (I, II Timothy, and Titus) should probably be regarded as non-Pauline letters. These are, in a sense, the earliest "commentaries" on Paul, insofar as they represent the attempts of later writers to interpret and apply the Pauline teaching to needs and situations the Apostle himself had not confronted and could not have foreseen. Opinions vary on how well these interpreters did their job and on how much they may have altered, rightly or wrongly, Paul's most fundamental convictions. We shall need to make at least a provisional decision about them, however, because they contain passages that often play a major role in discussions about Paul's view of women.

In this book these letters are not regarded as Paul's own. The arguments against Pauline authorship are given in the commentaries on Colossians and Ephesians listed at the end of chapter 2 and in the commentaries on the Pastoral Epistles listed at the end of this one. Even those who are not persuaded by these arguments should be aware of the problematic nature of their results when they include the disputed letters as evidence for Paul's views on any subject. The letters that most Pauline scholars agree are certainly the Apostle's own (Romans, I and II Corinthians, Galatians, Philippians, I Thessalonians, Philemon) provide the most secure information about Paul's mission and message. These must always be given the major weight in any exposition of his concrete ethical teaching. However, because I Timothy, Ephesians, and Colossians are so often cited for Paul's view of women in the church, we must pay some attention to the relevant passages in them as well. To these we shall add I Corinthians 14:33b-36, which stands in an authentic letter but may itself be non-Pauline.

1. I Timothy

The important passage for our topic is 2:8-15. In the preceding verses (2:1-7) instructions had been given about public prayer, what it should include and why it is important. Then in verse 8 the author enjoins the *men* to pray with uplifted hands (as was traditional in the Jewish synagogues) and "without anger or quarreling." As for the *women,* they should

> adorn themselves modestly and sensibly in seemly apparel, not with braided hair or gold or pearls or costly attire but by good deeds, as befits women who profess religion. Let a woman learn in silence with all submissiveness. I permit no woman to teach or to have authority over men; she is to keep silent. For Adam was formed first, then Eve; and Adam was not deceived, but the woman was deceived and became a transgressor. Yet woman will be saved through bearing children, if she continues in faith and love and holiness, with modesty. (I Tim. 2:9-15)

There is nothing specifically Christian about these comments on women. They could have been written by a Hellenistic Jew or—save for the reference to Adam and Eve—by any "secular" moralist of Paul's day. It was a commonplace among the ethical teachers of the Greco-Roman world that women should groom themselves modestly and refrain from public displays of any kind. To do otherwise would either mark them as women of easy virtue or else lead them to become such. A few examples will suffice to make the point.

Neopythagoreanism was a movement with philosophical and ethical interests which dated from the first century B.C. and reflected the influence of various older teachings and traditions. One ethical treatise that originated in this movement maintained that

> women who eat and drink all sorts of extravagant dishes and dress themselves sumptuously, wearing things that women are given to wearing, are decked out for seduction into all manner of vice, not

only the bed but also the commission of other wrongful deeds. . . .
The beauty that comes from wisdom and not from these things
brings pleasure to women who are well born.

Plutarch's "Advice to Bride and Groom" has already been
quoted in chapter 2. In the same essay he argued that a woman's
speech can be as seductive as her physical appearance:

> Not only the arm of the virtuous woman, but her speech as well,
> ought to be not for the public, and she ought to be modest and
> guarded about saying anything in the hearing of outsiders, since it
> is an exposure of herself; for in her talk can be seen her feelings,
> character and disposition. (142B)

A bit later he advises, "A woman ought to do her talking either to
her husband or through her husband" (142D, 32). An ancient
Latin dictum that asked specifically, "What have women to do
with a public assembly?" went on to supply the answer: "If
old-fashioned custom is preserved, nothing."

Similar teachings are present in the rabbinic traditions of
Judaism, specifically with reference to the participation of
women in public prayers. For such prayer a quorum was
necessary, and for this *minyan,* as the quorum was called, ten
adult males had to be present. A woman's presence was
allowed; but since she was under no obligation to participate,
her presence did not count. And she was *not* permitted to lead in
the prayers. Rather, the rabbis taught that her place was to
develop an inner spirituality, and they insisted that her primary
role was a domestic one. In the setting of the home she had the
chief responsibility for the children's instruction, but when she
was in the synagogue among the men she was to keep quiet.

It should be apparent that the comments about women in I
Timothy 2:8-15 reflect the values and customs of both
Hellenistic and Jewish culture. In addition, it is probable that the
Christian author of I Timothy was intent on refuting an aberrant
form of Christianity that, like some Corinthian Christians in

Paul's day, promoted rigidly ascetic ideas about Christian behavior. Consider, in this light, the author's remarks about women bearing children. His point would not be that a woman's only proper role is to satisfy her husband's desires and to produce babies. His comment would be a defense of the legitimacy of marriage, sex, and the family within the Christian community. As such, it would be a defense of women themselves, albeit in terms of the domestic role society in general and Judaism in particular had traditionally assigned to them.

2. Ephesians and Colossians

Although nothing is said in Ephesians and Colossians about the role of women in the church, these letters are often cited in confirmation of the view that women are to be subordinate to men in all ways and in every sphere of activity, including the church. The texts quoted are Ephesians 5:22-24 ("Wives, be subject to your husbands, as to the Lord," verse 24) and Colossians 3:18 ("Wives, be subject to your husbands, as is fitting in the Lord"). When Josephus sums up the Jewish view of marriage, the tradition lying behind these admonitions becomes clear: "The woman, says the Law, is in all things inferior to the man. Let her accordingly be submissive, not for her humiliation, but that she may be directed; for the authority has been given by God to the man" (*Against Apion,* 201).

The texts cited from Ephesians and Colossians stand within passages that scholars describe as "tables of household duties," or family codes. These speak not only about the responsibilities of wives to husbands, but also about the responsibilities of husbands to wives (Eph. 5:25-33; Col. 3:19), of children to parents (Eph. 6:1-3; Col. 3:20) and parents to children (Eph. 6:4; Col. 3:21), and of slaves to masters (Eph. 6:5-8; Col. 3:22-25) and masters to slaves (Eph. 6:9; Col. 4:1). The principle of mutual responsibility that Paul had stressed must operate between husbands and wives (I Corinthians 7) has been extended in Ephesians and Colossians to apply to other kinds of relationships as well. In both of these later writings this mutuality is grounded in the common status of all family members as persons in Christ, responsible finally to God alone. For example, the whole list of family duties in Ephesians is prefaced with the injunction, "Be subject to one another out of reverence for Christ" (5:21). It is the *codification* and *expansion* of Paul's own teaching which characterizes these various post-Pauline codes (in addition to those in Ephesians and Colossians, see especially I Pet. 2:11–3:12). The codification systematizes and generalizes Paul's teaching, and the expansion enables it to cover more cases.

In the ethical codes of such writings as Ephesians, Colossians, and I Peter, and in the rules and regulations of the Pastoral Epistles, we see a concern for social institutions and structures, political, ecclesiastical and domestic, that surpasses anything in Paul's own letters. These later writers did not share Paul's sense of the imminent close of history. They were reckoning with an indefinite delay in Christ's return and were concerned to help the church and individual Christians settle down in society. It was perhaps natural, given the political, social, and ecclesiastical pressures that confronted them, that their initial impulses were conservative. They were third-generation Christians. The pioneers in the faith were gone, and theirs was a time that required "regrouping" around the traditions they had received. It required them to think hard about the meaning of those traditions for their life in a world that did not appear to be "passing away" very quickly. They were having to grapple, as Paul himself had not, with the problem of a "social ethic." Perhaps they may be pardoned if they did not always clearly perceive the distinction between accommodation to the realities of the world and capitulation to its values and claims. We can gratefully receive these later writings as an important part of our Christian heritage. Let us not, however, confuse their teachings with those of the Apostle, whose moral instruction they themselves sought to interpret.

3. I Corinthians 14:33*b*-36

In chapters 11 through 14 of this letter, Paul is instructing the Corinthians to maintain order in their worship. Beginning in chapter 12, the matter of spiritual gifts is of special concern because of a dispute in the Corinthian congregation about speaking in tongues. This is still the subject in chapter 14. Paul's overall conclusion is that speaking in tongues is permissible but less edifying to the church than prophesying, which is the gift of intelligible speech (see, for instance, 14:39). And if there is to be speaking in tongues, he warns, it must proceed in orderly fashion and always with an interpreter (14:27-28). This, like all else in the Christian community, "should be done decently and in order" (14:40).

Near the end of this discussion stand the words about women in church, which the RSV, like many other versions, prints as a separate paragraph:

> (33*b*) As in all the churches of the saints, (34) the women should keep silence in the churches. For they are not permitted to speak, but should be subordinate, as even the law says. (35) If there is anything they desire to know, let them ask their husbands at home. For it is shameful for a woman to speak in church. (36) What! Did the word of God originate with you, or are you the only ones it has reached?

There are two striking things about this paragraph. First, it disrupts the flow of Paul's argument. Immediately before it and after it he is discussing the relative merits of prophecy and tongue-speaking. Several ancient manuscripts of I Corinthians remove verses 34-35 to the end of the chapter, showing that some early scribes were also puzzled about their appropriateness just here. Second, this admonition that women should not

91

talk in church and should rely on their husbands to explain things at home sounds very much like the teaching of I Timothy 2:11-12 and the tradition of which it is a part. It is not what one would expect to come from someone who, like Paul earlier in this same letter, was concerned to emphasize the equality of husbands and wives in marriage.

Indeed, many commentators believe that the verses before us (or at least verses 34-35) were not written by Paul. On this view, they may have originated as the marginal notation of some later scribe who, recalling the instruction of I Timothy 2:11-12 and finding nothing comparable in I Corinthians, added a similar provision near the end of Paul's discussion of Christian worship. In time, yet another scribe, using this manuscript as his master copy, could have mistaken the marginal notation for something that had been left out of his exemplar. By dutifully inserting it in the body of the text in his own copy, it thus became a part of I Corinthians! This is one of the ways an "interpolation" of later material could have occurred.

Several additional points lend support to the hypothesis that these verses constitute a non-Pauline interpolation. The expression "are not permitted" seems to look backward to a regulation previously formulated (for instance, in I Tim. 2:12); it is not Paul's way of phrasing his ethical teaching. The expression "be subordinate" echoes the stereotyped formula we have seen in the family codes of Ephesians and Colossians. Finally, but certainly not least, these verses contradict I Corinthians 11:2-16, where, as we shall see, Paul presumes not only that women may speak during public worship, but that they participate on an equal footing with men in both the prayers and the prophesying.

Galatians 3:27-28

Where shall we turn for firm evidence of Paul's teaching about women in the church? The passage with which to begin is unquestionably one in his letter to the Galatians, the two famous sentences in 3:27-28: "For as many of you as were baptized into Christ have put on Christ. There is neither Jew nor Greek, there is neither slave nor free, there is neither male nor female; for you are all one in Christ Jesus."

Paul is probably quoting or alluding to a traditional affirmation in the church's baptismal liturgy. The same formula is echoed in Romans 10:12, I Corinthians 12:13, and Colossians 3:11. In Galatians it is used as part of his argument that Christ frees one from the law and enables one, by faith, to become a child of God. The statement that immediately precedes the baptismal formula suggests what may have called it to his mind in this context: "For in Christ Jesus you are all sons of God through faith" (Gal. 3:26). *In* Christ Jesus—that is, in the community of faith—*all* believers are "sons of God." (What may sound like sexist language to modern ears would not have sounded so to Paul; with reference to God's people, Paul uses "son/sons" and "child/children" quite interchangeably, as in this very passage in 4:1-7.) Baptism into Christ means that all worldly distinctions become irrelevant. What is important before God is not whether one is Jew or Greek, slave or free, male or female. What is important above all is that one is "in Christ" and has "put Christ on."

The Apostle does not presume that these distinctions are erased. As a Christian, one necessarily retains one's ethnicity (Jew, Greek) and sexuality (male, female). As for legal status, Paul recognized that one's condition as "slave" or "free" was not necessarily permanent in Roman society. In I Corinthians 7:21 he counseled slaves to gain their freedom if possible, and he himself wrote to Philemon in an effort to get Onesimus his freedom. But "in Christ" it does not matter that one is a slave, because "in Christ" one's social class is of no more consequence than one's race or sex.

It is not a coincidence that the same baptismal affirmation is

93

reflected in I Corinthians 12:13 when Paul begins to develop his image of the church as the "body of Christ" (12:12-27). This imagery provides us a closer look at what he understands the traditional formula to mean. It means that those who are baptized into Christ, though they have different gifts, are bound together in their dependence on the same God (12:4-11). It means that though they serve in diverse ways they all "have the same care for one another" (12:25). It means, because the body cannot function without all its parts, that what the world values as "honorable" or what it rejects as "inferior," "weak," or "unpresentable" does not matter; all the members of Christ's body are equally valued as "indispensable" to its life (12:14-26).

But is it not significant, someone may ask, that Paul omits the reference to male and female equality in Christ when he uses the baptismal formula in I Corinthians 12:13? Doesn't this show that he is not really committed to it? The omission is significant, but not because of any doubts in Paul's mind about the full partnership of men and women in the body of Christ. The omission probably results from the state of affairs in the Corinthian congregation. In chapter 2 we saw that some Corinthian Christians believed their commitment to Christ required them to abstain from marriage and sex altogether. Such a view might have been prompted in the first place by the principle that "there is neither male nor female." Even if it had not, for Paul to repeat it now might only support one of the errors he wants to correct. Paul himself certainly did not interpret that principle to require the denial of one's sexuality. Therefore, its omission from the letter to Corinth perhaps shows how *seriously* the Apostle takes it, and how intent he is on preventing its misuse.

In his discussion of the diversity of gifts and functions in I Corinthians 12, there is not the slightest suggestion that one's racial or ethnic origin, one's position in the class structure, or one's being a man or a woman is in any way involved. There, by his allusion to the baptismal formula of Galatians 3:27-28, he is affirming without compromise the principle that all are one in Christ. But does he honor this principle in his own concrete ethical teaching? Our answer to this question must come from yet another passage in I Corinthians.

I Corinthians 11:2-16

Paul's instructions to the Corinthians on "good order in public worship" really begin in I Corinthians 11:2 and extend clear through chapter 14 of the letter. His advisories about their common meal (the Lord's Supper) in 11:17 ff. and about spiritual gifts in chapters 12–14 are well known. We tend to be much less familiar with the opening paragraphs, 11:2-16. This is not surprising, because Paul's concern here seems remote, even somewhat ridiculous, to the modern reader. He is explaining to the Christian women of Corinth why it is proper for them to cover their heads when they participate in worship.

The discussion opens with a commendation of the Corinthians for maintaining "the traditions" Paul has delivered to them. The plural form, "traditions," shows he is not thinking of the fundamental apostolic tradition, which he will later summarize in 15:3-5: "that Christ died for our sins . . . , that he was buried, that he was raised on the third day . . . and that he appeared to Cephas, then to the twelve." Rather, in 11:2-16 he is thinking of the ordinary and familiar ways of doing things in church. As he closes this first subtopic he refers specifically to what the established custom (RSV: "practice") is in "the churches of God" (verse 16), including (he hopes) the church in Corinth.

Paul's initial commendation of the Corinthians for maintaining the worship customs is immediately qualified, however. In one particular there is reason for concern. At least some of the women of their congregation have been going to church

95

bareheaded. This is indicated first of all in verse 6, only after Paul has started to develop his argument in favor of the usual practice: "any woman who prays or prophesies with her head unveiled dishonors her head—it is the same as if her head were shaven." The following verses confirm that this is the point at issue. Paul's arguments in favor of a woman's wearing some kind of head covering are varied and complex. In at least one instance, the argument that women should be veiled "because of the angels" (verse 10), scholars have made several different proposals about Paul's meaning, none of them fully convincing. Readers may consult the commentaries for discussion of this and many other points in the passage which cannot be treated here.

Our special concern is whether Paul's concrete teaching about women in the church corresponds to his espousal of the principle that "there is neither male nor female" in Christ. Although there are many details in I Corinthians 11:2-16 hard to explain, several things relevant to our study can be established with some degree of confidence. The conclusion to which they lead may be summarized as follows: Paul's arguments in this passage are *not* addressed to the question of the role or function of women in the church, not even in the church at Corinth. They were formulated for a much more specific objective and do not imply any general theory of woman's subordination to man. Moreover, the principle "there is neither male nor female" is visible in this very context, in what is said as well as in what is presumed. The evidence for this conclusion may be presented under four points.

(1) Paul is exercised about head coverings for the women in Corinth because of the more fundamental theological issue he is facing in that congregation.

One must realize that Paul has no special crotchet about women veiling their heads. It is something he believes ought to be taken for granted. It is not his innovation but a part of his culture. In Judaism it was strictly forbidden that a woman should

96

be seen in public with an uncovered head. Thus, a late-first-century rabbi was once asked, "Why does a man go out bareheaded while a woman goes out with her hair covered?" In non-Jewish circles as well it was commonly believed to be immodest for a woman to go about bareheaded. Plutarch, upon whose observations of first-century life we have relied in other connections, also provides some information on this topic. Describing Roman customs (which would also have prevailed in Corinth after its refounding as a Roman colony in 44 B.C.) he observes that "it is more usual for women to go forth in public with their heads covered and men with their heads uncovered" ("The Roman Questions," 267A).

This well-established custom seems as "natural" to Paul as women's long hair and men's short hair (I Cor. 11:14-15). Then why is there a problem in the church of Corinth? The failure of some (or most? or all?) of the women there to cover their heads for worship is perhaps one specific manifestation of the troublesome Corinthian religiosity. We have already seen how the extreme claims being made about the complete "spirituality" of the life in Christ could, and apparently did, lead some in Corinth to draw ascetic or libertinistic conclusions. Paul might easily suppose that the abandonment of the veil by women in church was another attempt to deny their sexual identity, another sign that they had misunderstood the principle, "there is neither male nor female." We may compare the remark of Lucian, a non-Christian writer of the second century A.D., about "a woman with her hair closely clipped in the Spartan style, boyish-looking and quite masculine" (*The Runaways,* 27). Thus, Paul's instruction in these verses is a very traditional one and seems to reflect his concern for the special theological confusion that marks the congregation in one city.

(2) Paul's theme here is the differentiation of one sex from the other, not the subordination of one sex to the other.

The argument of verses 3 through 9 needs to be observed with some care:

> (3) But I want you to understand that the head of every man is Christ, the head of a woman is her husband, and the head of Christ is God. (4) Any man who prays or prophesies with his head covered dishonors his head, (5) but any woman who prays or prophesies with her head unveiled dishonors her head—it is the same as if her head were shaven. (6) For if a woman will not veil herself, then she should cut off her hair; but if it is disgraceful for a woman to be shorn or shaven, let her wear a veil. (7) For a man ought not to cover his head, since he is the image and glory of God; but woman is the glory of man. (8) (For man was not made from woman, but woman from man. (9) Neither was man created for woman, but woman for man.)

One's initial impression is apt to be that Paul is arranging "God-Christ-husband-woman" in a hierarchical order moving from superior to inferior, each member subordinate to and controlled by the preceding. This impression is probably fostered most of all by the husband-woman part of the set and the fact that the subordination motif is so familiar to us from the family codes of Hellenistic Judaism and the later New Testament epistles. We are thus inclined to understand the headship metaphor as emphasizing the authority that the superior member exercises over the inferior. However, there are reasons to think that the authority-subordination theme is not primary in Paul's mind.

(a) Earlier in this same letter the formula, "you are Christ's; and Christ is God's" (3:23) had been used to complete and in a sense support the claim, "all things are yours" (3:21-22). Paul was affirming that the one who belongs to Christ and through him to God is no longer in bondage to anyone ("whether Paul or Apollos or Cephas") or to anything ("or the world or life or death or the present or the future"). In 11:3 the "you" of the earlier formula has been differentiated into male and female for the purposes of the argument about women's head coverings. The original affirmation about the sovereignty of God, which relativizes all other claims, is still implicit, however. Indeed, it becomes explicit in 11:12*b,* "And all things are from God."

(b) The Greek word "head" may be used metaphorically, as in English, to mean "one who is in charge." But it may also be used as a metaphor to designate "source" or "point of origin" (as in the English term "headwaters"). This second meaning, as Robin Scroggs has suggested, seems to be the one present in I Corinthians 11. Paul's comment in verses 8-9 that woman was created from and for man, not the reverse, shows that he is thinking of Genesis 2:18-23. There it is said that God took a rib from man's side and fashioned a woman from it to be like him. The Genesis story itself does not speak of woman's inferiority or subjection to man. It emphasizes, on the contrary, her being "like him." It says that she was created from his own flesh and bone in order to be his companion, because he was lonely. It does not say or suggest that she was created because man needed someone over whom to exercise control. *Derivation from* does imply *dependence upon,* in Genesis 2 and also in I Corinthians 11. But the kind of dependence involved in these cases is ennobling rather than demeaning. This will become clearer in the next point.

(c) In verse 7 the dependency scheme is restated substituting the words "image" and "glory" for "head." In this context Paul has no interest in belaboring the role of Christ, so now the set is abbreviated to "God-man-woman." This allows the Apostle to give closer attention to the issue he is addressing as well as to the scriptural passages upon which his argument is based. His reference to man as "the image and glory of God" derives specifically from Genesis 1:27, which states that "God created man in his own image, in the image of God he created him; male and female he created them." Modern students of the Bible recognize two different creation stories in Genesis, and Paul has drawn indiscriminately from both of them. In verses 8-9, as noted above, Paul alludes to the account in Genesis 2, according to which man was created first and then woman was formed later from his side. According to Genesis 1, however, male and female originated in the same creative act of God. Paul functions here as a good rabbinical interpreter of scripture, not as a modern biblical critic. In conflating the two different accounts, however, he misses an important point. In Genesis 1:27 "man" is a generic term, so when the text affirms "man's" creation in God's image the reference is to male and female alike. But Paul, influenced also by the text in Genesis 2, thinks only of the male as bearing the image and glory of God. He writes of the woman that "she is the glory of man" (I Cor. 11:7). Paul obviously wants to stress the *distinction* between male and female, and this accords with his concern that in their religious frenzy the Corinthians have been ignoring it. He refrains from drawing any wide-ranging conclusions about women's subjection to men, however. His one conclusion is that women should keep their heads covered when they are in church.

(3) In the midst of this very discussion, Paul in effect reaffirms the principle that "there is neither male nor female."

Reference has already been made to the complexity of Paul's argumentation in I Corinthians 11:2-16. In the present discussion we have not even tried to follow it in detail because that would have involved us with problems of no particular importance to our main topic. One senses that Paul himself was not completely satisfied with his arguments, because at the end of his discussion he says, perhaps with some frustration, "If anyone is disposed to be contentious, we recognize no other practice, nor do the churches of God." In other words, women should worship with covered heads even if these arguments aren't convincing, because "that's the way it's done"! Moreover, at one point in the discussion the Apostle pauses momentarily for an important aside. In the RSV it is printed as a parenthetical remark, which in a sense it is. This does not mean that it is unimportant, however. Precisely *because* it does not help Paul build his case against bareheaded women in church, it is all the more significant that Paul includes it. "Nevertheless, in the Lord woman is not independent of man nor man of woman; for as woman was made from man, so man is now born of woman. And all things are from God" (11:11-12).

That introductory "Nevertheless" breaks into the discussion like a cool evening breeze. It signals a point, not itself at issue, that Paul can unconditionally affirm and that he believes must stand even though all his intricate arguments may fall: the interdependence of man and woman and their common dependence upon the sovereign God. Here, as very often in his letters, we find the Apostle simultaneously indebted to the tradition in which he stands and concerned to correct it. When he says that "woman is not independent of man" and that "woman was made from man" he is repeating the tradition rooted in Genesis 2, just as he had done earlier in verses 8-9. But when he adds that "man [is not independent] of woman" and that "man is now born of woman," he is in effect correcting that tradition—or at least guarding against its misuse—by invoking the principle that "there is neither male nor female." In the very next chapter of this letter Paul will be emphasizing the unity that must prevail in the body of Christ. Its members, though differentiated by their gifts and their functions as well as by their race, sex, and social standing, are one in Christ. Their oneness and consequent interdependence are rooted in their common dependence upon God and faith in Christ. That principle had been distilled in the baptismal formula of Galatians 3:27-28, and it is reflected also in I Corinthians 11:11-12.

(4) Paul's entire discussion in this passage presumes that women as well as men participate in the leadership of public worship.

No arguments are advanced in support of the equality of

women and men in leading worship because they are not needed. Paul takes this for granted and must know that the Corinthians do too. This important presupposition of the passage is apparent in verses 4-5 where Paul phrases his remarks about a man and a woman in exactly parallel ways: "any man who prays or prophesies . . . , any woman who prays or prophesies. . . ." The issue is not whether a woman *may* utter prayers and prophecies in public worship, but only whether her head should be covered when she *does.*

There is nothing in the teaching of I Corinthians 11:2-16 that is incompatible with Paul's espousal elsewhere of the principle that "there is neither male nor female." Only if one approaches this passage as if it were a family code comparable to those in Ephesians and Colossians and applies Paul's arguments to subjects for which they were not devised will he be found deserting that principle. In fact, however, the presupposition of the whole discussion is that women can and do share fully in the leadership of worship. When we add our findings about this passage to our findings about Paul's remarks concerning the role of women in marriage relationships, it is clear that there is nothing in his teaching that compromises the affirmation of Galatians 3:27-28.

But does Paul adhere to his own teaching? What about his own practice? This will be the acid test of the depth of his conviction.

Women in Paul's Ministry

We know next to nothing about the women in Paul's family. There is only the notice in Acts 23:16 that "the son of Paul's sister" alerted the Apostle to the plot of some Jews to assassinate him. Of his own mother we know nothing. If he was ever married it was before his conversion, because he implies in I Corinthians 9:5 that he had not been "accompanied by a wife" during his apostolic ministry. The domestic side of Paul's life, therefore, gives us no inkling of Paul's relationships with or attitudes toward women.

On the other hand, we are fortunate in being able to piece together a good deal of information about Paul's dealings with women in the church. For this we shall rely chiefly on passages in his letters where specific women are mentioned. What emerges is the picture of an apostle who in practice as well as in principle supports the view that in Christ Jesus "there is neither male nor female."

1. Chloe

Paul's opening appeal in I Corinthians is that the dissensions and disagreements that have fractured the Corinthian congregation be overcome (1:10). In the next sentence he indicates the source of his information about the present difficulties: "For it has been reported to me by Chloe's people that there is quarreling among you" (1:11). The reference is literally to "those who belong to Chloe," and these could have been family members, friends, or slaves. The name itself tells us that Chloe was a woman. Obviously, she is someone known to the Corinthians as well as to Paul. Perhaps Chloe herself was a member of the Corinthian church, one of those widows Paul advises to remain as they are (I Cor. 7:8, 39b-40a). Or perhaps, since Paul is writing this letter from Ephesus, Chloe lived there and her "people" had been in Corinth on business. It is inherently more probable that Chloe was a Christian than that she was not, and it would appear that her standing with the Corinthian church and with Paul was such that both they and he knew a report from her "people" deserved to be taken seriously.

2. Euodia and Syntyche

The church at Philippi had been founded by Paul and his subsequent relationship to the Philippian congregation remained warm and cordial. According to Acts 16:11-15, Paul had preached first to some women of the city; and one of them, Lydia, was baptized by him. Her home, we are told, became a hospice for Paul and his companions. The same narrative goes on to say that after he and Silas were miraculously released from jail, Paul made it a point to visit Lydia before leaving the city (Acts 16:40). Yet Paul himself never mentions this person, and, as so often in the case of the stories in Acts, we are left wondering about the reliability of the information.

Two other women of Philippi are mentioned by Paul himself, however. In a letter to the Philippians he writes:

> I entreat Euodia and I entreat Syntyche to agree in the Lord. And I ask you also, true yokefellow, help these women, for they have labored side by side with me in the gospel together with Clement and the rest of my fellow workers, whose names are in the book of life. (4:2-3)

There are several things here one could wish to know more about. What was the matter about which these two women, Euodia and Syntyche, disagreed? It is idle to speculate. Who is the "true yokefellow" whom Paul urges to step in and help settle the dispute? We do not know. Nor do we have any idea who Clement is, save for what is indicated right here. The name appears nowhere else in Paul's letters or in Acts. Despite such unanswered questions as these, the verses do tell us some important things about women in Paul's ministry.

First, the disagreement between Euodia and Syntyche was of enough consequence to prompt Paul to give it specific attention, to name the disputants and to address them each individually, and to call upon a third party to help effect a reconciliation. This ought not to be shrugged off as "just a case of two bickering women" and used as the basis for another "Ladies' Aid" joke. Paul believes it to be a serious matter for the whole congregation. This by itself suggests that the women involved may have held positions of special responsibility in their church.

Their importance in Philippi is confirmed when Paul says that the two of them have "labored side by side . . . in the gospel" both with himself and "with Clement and the rest of my fellow workers." Whenever Paul speaks of laboring "in the gospel" he is speaking of his own apostolic ministry (Rom. 1:9; II Cor. 10:14) or of the ministry of his closest associates (of Timothy in I Thess. 3:2 and of an unnamed brother—Apollos?—in II Cor. 8:18). It is no insignificant thing for Euodia and Syntyche to be included in this company. Moreover, Paul makes it a point to indicate that their labor for the gospel has been no less important than that of "Clement and the rest." Although we cannot know anything specific about these persons, the reference to their names being "in the book of life" suggests they may have been early leaders of the Philippian church now deceased, but still remembered for their illustrious service "in the gospel."

As little as we know about Euodia and Syntyche, then, it is still enough to permit us the conclusion that they were important leaders of the Philippian congregation. It is enough to show us that Paul himself respected them as such, just as he regarded them along with men like Timothy and Clement as fully engaged in the ministry of the gospel.

3. Prisca (Priscilla)

Our evidence suggests that the woman closest to Paul was the one he calls Prisca and whose name appears in the alternate form "Priscilla" in the Book of Acts. She was married to Aquila who, according to Acts 18:2, was "a native of Pontus," a Roman province in northern Asia Minor on the Black Sea. There is no reason to doubt the further report in Acts that this couple had for a while resided in the capital of the Empire, but then removed to Corinth when the Emperior Claudius "commanded all the Jews to leave Rome" (18:2). The year would have been A.D. 49 when, as scholars have deduced from other ancient sources, the Jewish community in Rome was "in tumult" because of the presence among them of some believers in Christ. By no means "*all* the Jews" were expelled by Claudius, but the agitators certainly were. Maybe some other Jews or Jewish Christians fled the city at the same time.

Whether Prisca and Aquila were already Christians when they arrived in Corinth, or whether they were converted there, perhaps by Paul himself, we do not know. That they did meet Paul in Corinth is likely (Acts 18:1-2), and they may have been associated with him in the same trade, as Acts also reports (18:3). Prisca and Aquila accompanied Paul when he went on to Ephesus, but they did not accompany him when he took ship from there for Caesarea (Acts 18:18-19). Their residence in Ephesus is confirmed in the earliest mention of them to be found in Paul's own letters. This comes in I Corinthians, written from Ephesus to the church in the city from which Prisca and Aquila had removed to Ephesus. Near the close of that letter Paul writes: "Aquila and Prisca, together with the church in their house, send you hearty greetings in the Lord" (16:19). The reference to "*their* house" sounds natural enough to us, but it would have sounded far less so in Paul's day. Both law and custom assigned to the male special rights and duties as the head of the household, and one might have expected Paul to refer to "the church in *Aquila's* house." That he uses instead the plural possessive, "their," may suggest something about Paul's view of the marriage itself as well as about his understanding of Prisca's importance as a leader in the church.

Paul's other reference to these two friends is more informative. It occurs in Romans 16:3-5 where, this time, Paul is sending his greetings to them and "the church in their house." "Greet Prisca and Aquila, my fellow workers in Christ Jesus, who risked their necks for my life, to whom not only I but also all the churches of the Gentiles give thanks; greet also the church in their house." There are several reasons why it is unlikely that chapter 16 in our "book" of Romans was originally part of the letter to Rome. One of them is that it would require us to believe this couple has now returned to the city they left in A.D. 49, yet we have no evidence from Acts or Paul's other letters that they ever did. But where they are as they receive these greetings is not important, anyway. Wherever it is, they are still leaders in a local congregation. Now we learn in addition, however, that they had "risked their necks" for the Apostle's life. For that, both Paul and the churches he has founded are profoundly grateful.

In what way had they "risked their necks" for Paul? We cannot even be certain whether the expression is meant literally or metaphorically, although something similar is said about Epaphroditus of Philippi, and that seems to be meant literally (Phil. 2:30). The most important thing is that husband and wife are both mentioned, and that both are included without any hesitation or any hint of a distinction as Paul's "fellow workers in Christ Jesus." Moreover, in mentioning these friends, Paul again departs from normal usage in his day by naming the wife before the husband. Prisca's name also stands first in two of the three places in Acts where both are mentioned. It would appear reasonable to suppose that Prisca was recognized not only by Paul but also by the later church as being the more important of the two.

One of the instances in Acts where Aquila's name is preceded by his wife's is especially interesting. It is reported that after Paul's departure from Ephesus the renowned and eloquent Apollos arrived in the city and began to preach (Acts 18:24-25). Prisca and Aquila heard him in the synagogue but must not have been entirely satisfied with the gospel he proclaimed. This, at least, is what the writer of Acts wants us to believe, because he says that "they took him and expounded to him the way of God more accurately" (18:26). "They" refers to Prisca and Aquila, and thus we are confronted with the remarkable picture of a woman (named first) and her husband engaged in the theological instruction of one of the most famous preachers of their day. The scene is in direct contradiction to the rule of I Timothy 2:12, which "permit[s] no woman to teach or to have authority over men"! It is difficult to know what factual basis there may be for this story. The writer of Acts, after the fashion of many ancient writers, tends to mold history and traditions in keeping with his own ideas and objectives. The Gospel of Luke is also from his hand, and there he shows a special interest in portraying the importance of the women around Jesus. Nevertheless, enough is known about Prisca from Paul's own comments about her to make this story in Acts believable. Its net effect, therefore, is to strengthen the impression that women held positions of importance and authority in the Pauline churches.

4. Phoebe

Another name on the roster of women in Paul's ministry is that of Phoebe. She is mentioned in Romans 16:1-2. "I commend to you our sister Phoebe, a deaconess of the church at Cenchreae, that you may receive her in the Lord as befits the saints, and help her in whatever she may require from you, for she has been a helper of many and of myself as well." Whether this chapter was part of Paul's original letter to Rome, or whether it was a separate note sent originally to some other church, perhaps Ephesus, as many believe, does not affect our discussion. In either case it (or some part of it) is Paul's letter of recommendation for Phoebe, introducing her and asking that she be received hospitably.

Cenchreae was one of the port cities of Corinth, and this mention of it shows there was a Christian congregation there as well as in Corinth proper. Phoebe, we are informed, was an official of the congregation there. The RSV calls her "a deaconess," but to be quite fair to Paul's Greek we should call her a "deacon." The masculine form is used, not the feminine, and it is therefore gratuitous to postulate a separate order of "deaconesses" in Paul's churches on the basis of this text. Not even the form of her title distinguishes her from her male counterparts! In Paul's letters "deacon" is often used nontechnically as a reference to "one who serves." Thus, the RSV uses the words "servant(s)" or "minister(s)" to translate it when it refers to Paul and other apostles in I Corinthians 3:5; II Corinthians 3:6; 6:4 (compare II Cor. 11:15, 23). In I Thessalonians 3:2 it describes Timothy's service of God. It is also used with reference to Christ's ministry, once explicitly (Rom. 16:8) and once by implication (Gal. 2:17, where the RSV translates it as "agent").

In Philippians 1:1 Paul addresses "all the saints in Christ Jesus who are at Philippi, with the bishops and deacons." These persons seem to exercise special offices within the congregation, and the reference to Phoebe as a "deacon of the church at Cenchreae" suggests the same for her. The word itself, however, gives us no clue as to the specific kind of responsibility she may have had as a deacon. More instructive is the concrete description of her as "a helper of many and of myself as well." The crucial term here is the one rendered "helper" by the RSV and "good friend" by the NEB and Today's English Version. None of these translations, however, does justice to the Greek word Paul has used. Etymologically it means "one who stands before," and in ancient Greek texts it is often applied to a presiding officer. It could also mean a "patron" or "benefactor," and there is evidence of its use to describe an officer in a religious association. In an inscription pertaining to one specific Hellenistic cult, the word stands first in a list of various cultic officers, the others being: chief priest, scribe, custodians, and trustees. Paul's use of a feminine form of this noun has no known precedent.

However we choose to translate the term in question, Phoebe turns out to have been someone of considerable importance both in her own church and in Paul's ministry. In Romans 16:2

109

he says that she has served "many," including himself. Perhaps we should think of her as a *patroness* or *benefactress,* including but not restricted to the concept "protectress" (Goodspeed's translation). She is commended to an unusually long list of persons (16:3-16), as would be appropriate for one setting out for strange and distant places. These Christian friends of Paul are being asked to welcome and support her on her mission—the nature of which, unfortunately, Paul does not indicate.

5. Some Other Women

Among those to whom Phoebe is commended in Romans 16 are several other women concerning whom Paul has high praise: Mary ("who has worked hard among you," 16:6); Tryphaena and Tryphosa, perhaps twin sisters ("workers in the Lord," 16:12); the "beloved Persis" (who has also "worked hard in the Lord," 16:12); the unnamed mother of Rufus ("his mother and mine," 16:13); Julia; and the sister of Nereus (16:15). When, finally, we note that Apphia is one of those Paul is addressing in Philemon (verse 2), our catalog of women mentioned by Paul is complete. Apphia may have been Philemon's wife, but that is not certain. It is certain that she was a prominent member in the congregation to which Paul is sending that letter.

Conclusion

We have seen that it is crucial, particularly on the subject of women in the church, to distinguish between the letters of indisputably Pauline origin and those of the Apostle's later interpreters, penned in his name. One cannot ignore the views and practices of those who came after Paul. Ephesians, Colossians, and the Pastoral Epistles are also part of the church's canon of scripture. But only when we have made all of the proper distinctions between Paul's letters and the late ones will we be able to interpret each one in terms of its own social, historical, and religious context. Apart from some brief suggestions about the needs of the churches for which the later ethical codes were formulated, our attention here has been focused on Paul's own view of women in the church. The results are clear.

1. *Paul was committed to the fundamental principle that "there is neither male nor female" in Christ Jesus.* This principle was based on his conviction, firmly held, that the believers' common dependence upon God's grace and their joint incorporation into Christ brought them into a new relationship to one another. Their new identity, and ultimately their only significant one, was now "in Christ." The racial, national, legal, and sexual identities were not destroyed, but they were transcended and their meaning was relativized. They continued to exist in the world as Jew or Greek, slave or free, male or female—and, one might add, as single or married, artisan or farmer, and so on. But even their continued existence in these roles was understood by Paul to be radically qualified and transformed by their new being "in Christ."

2. *There is nothing in Paul's concrete teaching on matters pertaining to women that is incompatible with the principle he had affirmed.* The main passage that has to be tested in this connection is I Corinthians 11:2-16, since it is often used in support of the view that women are to remain subordinate in all ways to men. We have seen, however, that one must consider the situation Paul was addressing in that passage and avoid applying his arguments to matters for which they were not formulated. When his own intentions there are honored and when his own words about the interdependence of man and woman are heeded, one sees that his concrete teaching not only accommodates but actually exhibits the principle that "there is neither male nor female" in Christ.

3. *There is ample evidence that the principle was affirmed by*

Paul not only in words but also in practice. There are women among his closest associates in the ministry and women among the most prominent leaders in his churches. Their gifts, functions, and accomplishments are in no way distinguishable because they are female. Such distinctions do exist within the body of Christ, but there is no hint that one's sex is tied up with them in any way. Paraphrasing Paul, one might ask: Must all apostles be Jewish? Must all prophets be Gentiles? Must all teachers be women? Must all helpers be slaves? Paul's response would be unequivocal: Of course not! The evidence from his letters is so overwhelming that one knows as soon as these questions have been formulated that they are ridiculous. On the topic of women in the church, certainly, Paul's principle was unambiguous: "There is neither male nor female." Not only was his teaching compatible with this, but his own practice was a demonstration of it.

For Further Reading

There are three excellent articles on "Woman" in *The Interpreter's Dictionary of the Bible,* Vol. 5, one dealing with the Ancient Near East (Rivkah Harris), another with the Old Testament (Phyllis Trible), and a third with the New Testament (Robin Scroggs). Each includes a bibliography.

Krister Stendahl's *Bible and the Role of Women,* Facet Books Biblical Series, 15 (Philadelphia: Fortress Press, 1966) is still useful despite its brevity and the fact it is now somewhat dated. A more recent study, which focuses on Paul specifically, is Elisabeth Schüssler Fiorenza's article, "Women in the Pre-Pauline and Pauline Churches," *Union Seminary Quarterly Review,* 33 (1978), 153-66.

There are numerous other articles and books in which Paul's teaching about women receives some attention, but not many of these have been written by biblical scholars. An important exception is the book by Evelyn and Frank Stagg noted at the end of chapter 2. While their discussion of the codes in Ephesians, Colossians, and other letters is excellent, their interpretation of I Corinthians 11:2-16 misses various points that I have suggested are crucial to a proper understanding of the teaching there.

Another husband-wife team, Richard and Joyce Boldrey, has devoted a whole book to the subject of Paul and women: *Chauvinist or Feminist: Paul's View of Women* (Grand Rapids: Baker Book House, 1976). Their entire approach is flawed, however, by their refusal to distinguish between the letters of certain and disputed Pauline authorship and by their quite uncritical use of materials from Acts. The analysis of specific passages is often unreliable, and not always informed by recent scholarship. The annotated bibliography contributed by David M. Scholer is worth consulting, however.

For general background information (apart from Judaism) the book of Sarah B. Pomeroy, *Goddesses, Whores, Wives, and Slaves: Women in Classical Antiquity* (New York: Schocken Books, 1975) is excellent; Flora Levin's translation of the Neopythagorean treatise from which I have quoted may be found there, pp. 134-36. Moshe Meiselman's *Jewish Woman in Jewish Law,* Vol. VI in The Library of Jewish Law and Ethics (New York: Ktav, 1978), may be consulted especially for the woman's role in public prayer.

Plutarch's "Roman Questions" is quoted from F. C. Babbitt's translation in The Loeb Classical Library, *Moralia,* IV (1936), and Lucian's *Runaways* is quoted from A. M. Harmon's translation in the same series, *Lucian,* V (1936).

Commentaries on I Corinthians are given at the end of chapter 2. Conzelmann's is particularly important on the question of 14:33b-36 and for its analysis of the argument in 11:2-16. I have quoted the Latin dictum on page 88 above according to the translation provided in the English edition of

Conzelmann's commentary, page 246, note 57. A number of interesting texts on women's hairstyles and head coverings in antiquity are gathered together on pages 185-86 of the same volume.

Commentaries on Romans are given at the end of chapter 3.

There are excellent commentaries on the Pastoral Epistles: M. Dibelius, rev. H. Conzelmann, trans. P. Buttolph and A. Yarbro for Hermeneia (Philadelphia: Fortress Press, 1972); F. D. Gealy, Exegesis in *The Interpreter's Bible,* Vol. 11 (Nashville: Abingdon, 1955); C. K. Barrett in the New Clarendon Bible series (Oxford: At the Clarendon Press, 1963); A. T. Hanson in the Cambridge Bible Commentary on the New English Bible series (Cambridge: At the University Press, 1966). The best commentary on Colossians is Eduard Lohse's, trans. W. R. Poehlmann and R. J. Karris for Hermeneia (1971). For Ephesians, F. W. Beare's exegesis in *The Interpreter's Bible,* Vol. 10 (1953) is still useful.

V

Christians and the Governing Authorities

The topics examined so far have kept our attention fixed primarily upon the Christian community itself and on problems of personal, family, and ecclesiastical morality. None of these spheres of moral concern is separable from the others, of course. Moreover, we have been reminded in various ways that Paul's moral instructions and advice were given and received in the still broader context of the Christian's life in "the world." It is appropriate, then, that our final probe of Paul's teaching should attempt to assess this dimension of his moral concern. We can do this best by posing the specific question of the Christian's obligations to the governing authorities. The passage that will have to claim our closest attention is Romans 13:1-7. These verses would certainly stand high on anyone's list of problem texts in Paul's ethical teaching. A consideration of them will afford an excellent opportunity to close this book as it opened—by emphasizing that Paul's moral instruction should not be regarded either as a sacred cow or as a white elephant.

The Pauline Principle

As in the case of the role of women in the church, so in the matter of the Christian's relation to "the world" and its various kinds of claims, Paul's principle would seem clear. Three famous

115

texts express it in different ways, but the underlying conception is the same in each instance.

He reminds the Philippians that the "state" (RSV translates "commonwealth") to which Christians belong "is in heaven," from whence they "await a Savior," their one true "Lord Jesus Christ" (Phil. 3:20). Christians are thus distinguished from those who have their "minds set on earthly things" (3:19).

We have already seen how Paul wrote to the Corinthians that "the form of this world is passing away," and that they should therefore regard all worldly institutions and claims as provisional only:

> From now on, let those who have wives live as though they had none, and those who mourn as though they were not mourning, and those who rejoice as though they were not rejoicing, and those who buy as though they had no goods, and those who deal with the world as though they had no dealings with it. (I Cor. 7:29-31)

The third text is one of the most fundamental of the Apostle's exhortations and serves to link the theological argumentation of the first eleven chapters of Romans to the ethical teaching of chapters 12 and 13.

> Therefore, my brothers, I implore you by God's mercy to offer your very selves to him: a living sacrifice, dedicated and fit for his acceptance, the worship offered by mind and heart. Adapt yourselves no longer to the pattern of this present world, but let your minds be remade and your whole nature thus transformed. Then you will be able to discern the will of God, and to know what is good, acceptable, and perfect. (Rom. 12:1-2 NEB)

This text, like those from Philippians and I Corinthians, is written with a keen sense that history is drawing to a close and that Christ's return is imminent. Elsewhere Paul says of "the end" that Christ "delivers the kingdom to God the Father after destroying every rule and every authority and power" (I Cor. 15:24), and that he "will change our lowly body to be like his

116

glorious body, by the power which enables him even to subject all things to himself" (Phil. 3:21). Can there be any question, then, about the implications of this for one's obligations to earthly rulers? Christians belong to another world, to the one Ruler above all earthly rulers, to the One to whom all earthly powers shall be put in subjection. Does not Paul himself show us what kinds of practical consequences follow from this when he tells the Corinthians not to take their disputes to the secular courts (I Cor. 6:1-6)? It would seem so—until one reads Romans 13:1-7 with its explicit admonition to "be subject to the governing authorities." Is this not a monumental contradiction of what seems, from other texts, to be a fundamental Pauline principle?

Romans 13:1-7

There have been times in the history of Christianity when this passage has been the victim of the sacred-cow approach to Paul's moral instruction. Thus, some Christians in Hitler's Germany appealed to it as the decisive biblical warrant for obedience to the Nazi regime. More recently, many American Christians invoked this text against those who refused to support their government's policies and actions in Vietnam. Indeed, as J. C. O'Neill has written, "These seven verses have caused more unhappiness and misery in the Christian East and West than any other seven verses in the New Testament" because of the support they have seemed to require for even tyrannical governments and unjust policies.

On the other side, what some have used as a sacred cow others have discarded as a white elephant. Paul has often been called naïve on this point; or else, granting its pertinence for his own time, the admonition of Romans 13:1-7 has been dismissed as outmoded for ours. There have even been some scholarly attempts to ease us out of this problem passage by denying that

117

Paul ever wrote it. The claim is that we have here another late interpolation into the text of a Pauline letter, a passage that not only interrupts the context but contradicts Paul's own conviction that the Christian's sole allegiance is to God. In another instance, I Corinthians 14:33*b*-36, we have seen good evidence of a later addition to a Pauline letter. There is no real evidence for a similar theory about Romans 13:1-7, however; the arguments rest entirely on conjecture and a strong feeling that Paul simply would not have required such obedience to political rulers. The vast majority of commentators are agreed that this passage must be considered part of Paul's own moral instruction, whether we like it or not.

We shall be aided in our analysis of the form and content of Romans 13:1-7 if we consider first the historical-social context from within which Paul approaches the matter, and then the literary-theological context of the passage in which his instructions are given.

1. The Historical-Social Context

Paul, born and reared a Jew, was influenced in various ways by the traditions, values, and teachings of Hellenistic Judaism in particular. We have seen examples of such influence in his instructions on marriage and divorce, in his attitudes toward homosexual behavior, and in his presumptions about the propriety of women's covering their heads in public. It is not unreasonable to suppose that his ideas about allegiance to political authorities will also show signs of his religious background in Judaism.

The Jews were no strangers to political crisis and to the potential conflict between allegiance to God and allegiance to earthly rulers. As a people they had experienced exile, persecution, political oppression and the indignities, intrigues, and terrors of life under puppet governments. In 200 B.C. Antiochus III, one of the Seleucid successors to Alexander the

Great, had wrested the control of Palestine away from the Ptolemies of Egypt, who had exploited both the land and its people. The Jews not unnaturally supported Antiochus against the Ptolemies, and in return the new government lessened the burden of taxation that had so vexed the Jews. In 190 B.C., however, Antiochus himself suffered a military defeat at the hands of the Romans in Asia Minor, and the Seleucids were forced to pay exorbitant reparations to Rome. To help, they imposed additional taxes on the Jews and even attempted—but failed—to appropriate the temple treasury in Jerusalem. The infamous Antiochus IV (Epiphanes) deposed the Jewish high priest in 175 B.C. and twice in succession sold the office to the highest bidder. When he sought to turn Jerusalem itself into a Hellenistic city, the Maccabees, a group of Jewish "freedom fighters," revolted (167 B.C.); and by 141 B.C. the Jews had their independence under the Hasmoneans, a new dynasty of high priests.

Roman control of Palestine dates from 63 B.C., when the Roman general Pompey intervened in a dispute between rival factions of the Hasmonean house. After several months of siege, Jerusalem fell, and all of Palestine was subsequently brought under Roman jurisdiction. A measure of independence was granted to the Jews by Augustus in 47 B.C., but under Herod, Rome's puppet-king in Palestine (37–4 B.C.), the Jews experienced a merciless despotism, which included the confiscation of property and the imposition of heavy taxes. The Herodian royal house retained some power in Palestine until A.D. 94, but always in uneasy tandem with imperial Rome, whose officers, like Pontius Pilate, who served in Judea from A.D. 26 to 36, were responsible directly to the emperor.

In 6 B.C. Judea was officially declared a Roman province, and over the next twelve years a group of Jewish revolutionaries, the Zealots, came into being. Zealotism was rooted in a zealous determination to adhere firmly and without compromise to the

Jewish law. The movement as such took shape, however, when Judas the Galilean departed from Pharisaism in general and proposed that the first of the Ten Commandments had a directly *political* application. "No other gods before me," he insisted, precluded any foreign rule over Israel. For example, if one pays taxes to the king, one breaks the law of God. From small-scale guerrilla operations against Roman military units in Palestine, Zealot activities escalated into a full-scale revolt in A.D. 66. Zealot forces freed Jerusalem from the occupying Romans and made sure to destroy the Roman archives there, including the tax records. Now the full might of Roman military force was felt in Palestine. It was all-out war. Then in A.D. 70 a Roman army under Titus recaptured the city after a bloody siege, killed many of its inhabitants, and burned the temple. The last Zealot forces retreated to the fortress at Masada, where in A.D. 73/74 they chose suicide over the alternative of surrender to the Romans.

Not all Jews shared the religious zeal and political objectives of the Zealots, however. Jewish scripture and tradition had generally taught that the governing authorities deserved respect. Jeremiah's letter to the exiles in Babylon laid upon them as God's own command the charge to "seek the welfare of the city where I have sent you into exile, and pray to the Lord in its behalf, for in its welfare you will find your welfare" (Jer. 29:7). One sees an emphasis on the importance of respect for earthly rulers in the Wisdom literature especially. Wisdom herself teaches, "By me kings reign, and rulers decree what is just; by me princes rule, and nobles govern the earth" (Prov. 8:15-16). Another proverb counsels, "My son, fear the Lord and the king, and do not disobey either of them" (Prov. 24:21).

The Wisdom of Solomon, an apocryphal book of the first century B.C., has already helped us follow Paul's thought in Romans 1:18-32. It can help us also on the subject of allegiance to governing authorities. The "kings," "judges," and "rulers" of the earth (Wisd. 6:1-2) are reminded, "your dominion was given you from the Lord, and your sovereignty from the Most High" (6:3). However, because "as servants of his kingdom [they] did not rule rightly, nor keep the law [of God]," swift and terrible judgment will come down upon them (6:4-8). All earthly rulers are warned, therefore, to "learn wisdom and not transgress" and to be instructed in holiness (6:9-11). Another document of Hellenistic Judaism of about the same date affirms that "it is God who bestows on all kings glory and great wealth, and no one is king by his own power" (*Aristeas* 224).

The Jewish Essene sect was a closed community devoted to the strict observance of the Mosaic Law, but did not draw the same political conclusions from it that their contemporaries, the Zealots, did. Rather, as Josephus tells us, every new member of the sect pledged to "forever keep faith with all men, especially with the powers that be, since no ruler attains his office save by the will of God" (*The Jewish War*, II, 140). From various sources we learn that even under Roman rule the Jews in general continued to offer sacrifices to God for the emperors and that in their synagogues most Jews continued to pray for the rulers and their welfare (for example, Philo's *Against Flaccus,* 48, 49; *Embassy to Gaius,* 279-80, 301, 305). And about the time that the Zealot party openly revolted against Rome, Rabbi Hanina was teaching his disciples, "Pray for the welfare of the government, for were it not for the fear of the government, a man would swallow up his neighbor alive."

A final example of Jewish custom in this matter is in a sense the most remarkable of all. Shortly after the accession of Gaius (Caligula) to the imperial throne in A.D. 37, a vicious pogrom was launched against the Jews of Alexandria, a city in the Roman province of Syria. Philo, the distinguished philosopher of that city, in the year 39 headed a delegation of Jews to go to Rome and plead with the Emperor for relief. Philo's essay, *Embassy to Gaius,* tells us about this mission and the events leading up to it. Philo was certainly not naïve about the injustice and evil that could be perpetrated by earthly rulers, especially by a madman like Gaius. But even as he tells about his mission to the imperial court, he continues to stress the point that the Jews "had a twofold motive, respectful fear of the emperor and loyalty to the consecrated laws" (236). The former was demonstrated when, as Philo tells it, he and his delegation were presented to the emperor: "the moment we saw him we bowed our heads to the ground with all respect and timidity and saluted him addressing him as Emperor Augustus" (352). The latter was demonstrated by the fact that the Jews offered sacrifices *for* Gaius at his accession but not *to* him. The distinction was a crucial one to the Jews, and that point was not lost on the emperor who therefore judged the sacrifices to be an inadequate sign of obeisance (356-57).

The apostle Paul could not have been a Christian very long when Philo was in Rome on his "embassy to Gaius." His missionary travels in Asia Minor and Greece were still in the future. Christianity was still a largely Palestinian and Jewish movement, probably regarded as an eccentric Jewish sect by any Gentile who happened to encounter or hear of it at all. Even with the establishment of Pauline congregations in such important cities as Ephesus, Miletus, Troas, Philippi, Thessalonica, and Corinth, the Christian church had an extremely low profile in the Greco-Roman world. The movement is barely mentioned in the non-Christian literature of the first century; if it was even known, it was dismissed as unimportant. And so it was, from a political point of view.

Occasionally, Christian evangelists and leaders had confrontations with Roman authorities at the local level, but this was not because of any active governmental program of repression or persecution. Not until the disastrous fire of Rome in the summer of A.D. 64, which Nero sought to blame on the Christians, was there concerted persecution of Christians (Paul himself was probably one of the victims), and even then it was local and temporary. The persecutions under Domitian some thirty years later were more serious, but Christianity as a movement was not outlawed until the edict of Diocletian in A.D. 303. Before then, Christians generally were safe from governmental interference unless accused of specific crimes; they were more the victims of informers than of the state itself. This is important to remember as we seek to recreate the political and social setting in which Paul wrote to the Roman Christians about being subject to the governing authorities. The year was most likely 56 or 57, still early in Nero's reign (A.D. 54–68), when there was considerable confidence abroad that his administration would be just and humane. The Great Persecution of the church was still centuries off.

2. The Literary-Theological Context

Romans 13:1-7 stands in the midst of a series of concrete ethical exhortations, which begin in 12:3 and end in 13:7. These exhortations are framed by the introductory appeal of 12:1-2 and the concluding appeals of 13:8-14.

The introductory appeal is of a very fundamental nature, as we have already had occasion to note. It urges Christians to offer themselves wholly and unreservedly to the spiritual worship of God. They are not to be conformed to this present age, but are to live rather as transformed and renewed persons within it, seeking out and doing God's holy will.

The concluding appeals serve as a summary of what had preceded. God's will is love; that is how all the law's commandments are fulfilled. The urgency of this is then underscored, as it had been at the beginning, by remarking that the Christian belongs to the New Age, not to the old. Now the symbolism of "night" and "day" is employed to express this. Because "the night is far gone" and "the day is at hand," Christians must "cast off the works of darkness and put on the armor of light," which is "the Lord Jesus Christ" himself.

The specific moral injunctions that are framed by these opening and closing appeals may themselves be divided into two main groups. The first group of injunctions applies to life within the body of Christ, the second to one's relationships with those outside the church. It is not completely agreed where the boundary line is between these two. Some place it before the exhortation of 12:14 to "bless those who persecute you," but others believe it should be placed in the middle of 12:16. On this latter view a new sentence and a new paragraph would open with the words, "Do not be haughty, but associate with the lowly. . . ." The "borderline verses," in other words, are 12:14-16a, but our present topic does not require us to settle the questions that have been raised about them. It is enough to observe that 13:1-7 not only belongs to the second group, but constitutes the lengthiest topic within it.

What is the theological context of these appeals in Romans 12 and 13? This is indicated first of all by the way they are introduced and concluded. In each case Paul emphasizes that the Christian's present life is radically qualified by the imminence of the New Age. He does not conclude from this, however, that those who in Christ belong to the New Age no longer have any responsibilities for the present age. On the contrary, his point is that the new life in Christ places special moral requirements upon the believer. The power of the New Age is already evident in the gifts with which the members of Christ's body have been individually endowed (12:3-8): gifts to prophesy, to serve, to teach, to exhort, to aid others, and to show mercy. These gifts are not to be retained as trophies of salvation (the Corinthian error) but are to be used for the service of God in the world. They are the means by which the believer's faith may be enacted in love.

Paul's discussion of spiritual gifts in I Corinthians 12 had led him to stress love as the fundamental claim of the new life in Christ (I Cor. 13; 14:1). Now here again, in Romans 12, his description of the spiritual gifts by which Christians are summoned to obedience is followed by a summary appeal to "let love be genuine" (verse 9a). From this point through verse 21, the individual admonitions spell out love's requirements to those inside and outside the Christian community. Then in 13:8-10 the love command reappears in the summary appeal of the whole section.

The theological context that is provided by the letter as a whole accords with that suggested by 12:1-2 and 13:8-14. All persons ("Jew and Gentile") stand in need of God's grace. Apart from that, the Gentile is enslaved "to a base mind and to improper conduct" (1:28), and the Jew is enslaved to a law that promises righteousness but actually opens the door to sin (for example, 2:17-24; 7:7-11). But those who by faith are united with Christ in his death have been freed from bondage through God's love, which is made effective there; and they have been brought instead under the rule of grace (5:6–7:6; 8:2-4). The "base mind" is now "renewed" and "transformed" for the service of God (12:2). The one true "law" is now understood to be the "law of love" (13:8-10), which derives from God's redemptive action in Christ (5:6-11; love is thus "the law of Christ," Gal. 6:2). In summary, the admonitions of Romans 12–13 illustrate how those whose lives have been transformed in Christ are to become "instruments of righteousness" (Rom. 6:13) wherever and however long in the present age it is given them to exist.

3. The Passage Itself

What theme or concern is common to 13:1-7 and its context in chapters 12 and 13? We have noted the importance of love in this context, and it is true enough that the various admonitions in 12:9-21 are all more or less derivative from the basic appeal of 12:9a to "let love be genuine." But those admonitions are rounded off in 12:21, "Do not be overcome by evil, but

overcome evil with good." Nothing in 13:1-7 suggests that Paul
is thinking of the governing authorities as an instance of "evil" or
of the Christian's subjection to them as the overcoming of evil
with good (love). Rather, Paul describes the governing authority
as "God's servant for your good" (13:4), and he identifies
"conscience," not the love command, as the basic reason to "be
subject" (13:5).

What does link 13:1-7 with its context in chapters 12 and 13 is
the concern to show how, even in the "secular" sphere, the
Christian must seek to do what is "good" according to God's
will. This is articulated in the introductory appeal of 12:2 ("to
discern the will of God, and to know what is good" NEB); it
resurfaces in 12:9*b* ("hate what is evil, hold fast to what is
good"), again in 12:17, 21 ("Repay no one evil for evil, . . . but
overcome evil with good"), and yet again in the midst of 13:1-7
("do what is good," 13:3*b*).

As we shall see, the topic in 13:1-7 is *not* "the state" and the
main appeal of these verses is *not* to "be subject" to it. The
admonition to "be subject" does open the paragraph (verse 1),
and it is repeated in verse 5. But these verses are preliminary to
the main appeal, which is to pay whatever kinds of taxes one
owes (verses 6, 7). Once this chief point has been made, Paul is
ready to summarize all the preceding instructions. He does this
by generalizing the appeal of 13:6-7 in such a way as to return to
the importance of love: "Owe no one anything, except to love
one another" (13:8).

Now we are able to examine this passage itself more closely. In
order to clarify the structure and progression of Paul's argument,
the seven verses may be subdivided into four groups. In verses 1
and 2 Paul is saying that the authority of the governing
authorities has been granted to them by God. The next thought,
verses 3-4, is that earthly rulers function as servants of God to
employ the authority granted them for the common good. Verse
5 advances a third point, and in doing so repeats the opening

admonition: one should "be subject" not only for fear of punishment, but "for the sake of conscience." Finally, in verses 6-7, it is said that, in the specific instance of taxes, one should comply with the demands of the governing authorities.

Here we have the gist of the passage, but obviously all of the really interesting and difficult questions remain to be answered. How does this accord with Paul's fundamental principle that one lives in the world but should not be of the world? Does Paul regard the Roman Empire as divine? Does he leave no room for "civil disobedience"? To get at these questions, we must examine in turn each of the four phases of the argument.

> Let every person be subject to the governing authorities. For there is no authority except from God, and those that exist have been instituted by God. Therefore he who resists the authorities resists what God has appointed, and those who resist will incur judgment. (13:1-2)

One should observe, first of all, that neither here nor elsewhere in this passage does Paul speak of "obeying" or "disobeying" the governing authorities. Instead, and in line with the tradition in which he stands, he speaks of being "subject" to them, the opposite of which is "resisting" them. Both words imply the existence of an orderly structure, in this case a political structure. The opposite of "subjection" is not so much "disobedience" as "disruption." To "be subject" means to acknowledge the reality of the political structure under which one stands, and to respect it. One might, for example, "disobey" a law of the state and still "be subject" to the political structure, namely, to the due processes and penalties administered in cases of disobedience.

In the second place, it should be carefully noted that there is nothing distinctively Pauline, or even distinctively Christian, in these first two verses. Two interrelated points are being made. First, earthly rulers have no authority except what God has given them; and second, whoever resists them is resisting God's authority and is liable to judgment. Paul has inherited both of these ideas from the traditions of Hellenistic Judaism, as a comparison with the various passages we have examined earlier will show. There is, for instance, the statement of Josephus when commenting on the Essene pledge that "no ruler attains his office save by the will of God." And the advice, "My son, fear the Lord and the king, and do not disobey either of them" (Prov. 24:21, distinctly echoed in a later Christian text, I Peter 2:17). It is crucial to realize that this same tradition held the earthly ruler accountable to God and emphasized that he himself was liable to God's judgment. For those who do not "walk according to the purpose of God," the judgment will be swift and severe, and it does not matter that they are among the high and the mighty; "a strict inquiry is in store for the mighty" (Wisd. 6:4-8). Their possession of authority is not to be construed as a sign of their inherent goodness and wisdom. Rather, it lays upon them the *responsibility* to "learn wisdom and not transgress," and to long for divine instruction in the ways of holiness (Wisd. 6:9-11).

> For rulers are not a terror to good conduct, but to bad. Would you have no fear of him who is in authority? Then do what is good, and you will receive his approval, for he is God's servant for your good. But if you do wrong, be afraid, for he does not bear the sword in vain; he is the servant of God to execute his wrath on the wrongdoer. (13:3-4)

The first point to notice in these verses is that Paul describes the governing authorities as God's *servants.* Neither here nor in verse 6, where he uses the synonymous expression, "ministers of God," does he imply that earthly rulers are the divine representatives of God on earth. They are here to *serve,* and the authority they hold is to be recognized not because it is theirs, but because it is not really "theirs" but has been given them by God. Both points are in accord with the presumption of the tradition in which Paul stands on this matter, that earthly rulers are responsible for governing wisely and justly.

The other important point in these verses is Paul's specification of the proper functions of the governing authorities. They are to support what is good, thereby assuring the welfare of the whole society. They are the administrators of civil justice (Paul isn't thinking about disputes within the church, as he is in I Cor. 6:1-6), not only punishing those who do wrong, but supporting those who work for what is good. Thus, the governing authorities are set here "for your good," Paul writes. If we are to believe the picture drawn for us by Acts, Paul had more than once been the beneficiary of the law and order that Roman civil and military authority had made a reality throughout the Mediterranean world, even though he had also been its victim. His own continuing confidence in the political system of his day was demonstrated when, sometime after the writing of this letter to the Roman Christians, having been arrested in Jerusalem and imprisoned in Caesarea, he appealed his case, as a Roman citizen, to the emperor (Nero) himself. World traveler that he was, Paul was doubtless more aware than the average person of the social, economic, and political stability that Roman rule had made possible even in the farthest reaches of the Empire. His thought in this passage is similar to that expressed by Rabbi Hanina (about A.D. 66), which was quoted earlier: "Were it not for the fear of the government, a man would swallow up his neighbor alive."

There has been much debate about the exact meaning of the reference here to the one who "does not bear the sword in vain." Is this a reference to the administration, in certain cases, of capital punishment by Roman tribunals? Or rather, to the military power of Rome, which Paul well knew was capable of putting down rebellion, keeping the sea lanes free of pirates and the highways free of brigands? The reference may be more specific than either of these, but further comment is best reserved until we have looked at the remaining verses, especially the last two.

Therefore one must be subject, not only to avoid God's wrath but also for the sake of conscience. (13:5)

The appeal to "be subject" with which this paragraph had opened (verse 1) is now repeated. But an important idea is also added in this verse. Until now, Paul's prime argument for being subject to the governing authorities has been that they are God's servants for the maintenance of law and order and the administration of justice. Now he says it is not only for this reason, but "for the sake of conscience" that one must be subject. "Conscience" is a term Paul seems to have picked up from the Corinthians, among whom it was popular. It was not a term that had currency in Hellenistic Judaism, and the appeal to conscience was therefore not a part of the tradition about subjection to earthly rulers on which Paul is otherwise dependent in this passage. Paul ordinarily thinks of one's conscience as that facility for engaging in the critical assessment of a course of action already taken or the critical reflection upon a course of action about to be taken. In this particular passage it seems to refer to one's capacity to reflect critically upon what is appropriate given the realities of existence in the world. Here Paul does not regard conscience as the mediator of any special "Christian truth." He means simply that, if one thinks reasonably and carefully about the matter at hand, subjection to the ruling authorities will commend itself as the wise and prudent way. But what, after all, is "the matter at hand"? If it were the abstract question of whether a Christian ought to "be subject" to the governing authorities the proper climax of this passage would have been reached here in the fifth verse: the charge is repeated, the power of rulers to enforce subjection is summarized, and there is a final appeal to one's "conscience." This verse does not conclude the discussion, however. It only sums it up to this point. The conclusion and the real point of the paragraph come in the next two verses.

> For the same reason you also pay taxes, for the authorities are ministers of God, attending to this very thing. Pay all of them their dues, taxes to whom taxes are due, revenue to whom revenue is due, respect to whom respect is due, honor to whom honor is due. (13:6-7)

Everything Paul has been saying in verses 1-5 has been leading up to the specific topic of "taxes," which emerges finally in these two verses. Paul has reminded his readers of their obligation to "be subject to the governing authorities" and of the reasons for that. In verse 6 he points out a specific way in which they are now fulfilling that obligation: by paying taxes. Finally, in verse 7, he indicates what they *should* do to fulfill their obligation. Some interpreters believe that there is an allusion here to the famous saying of Jesus that we know from the Synoptic Gospels and that Paul perhaps knew from the oral tradition: "Render to Caesar the things that are Caesar's, and to God the things that are God's" (Mark 12:17). We might have expected some explicit appeal to "the Lord's" authority, if that is what Paul is invoking (compare I Cor. 7:10), though it could be argued that Paul presumes his readers would be familiar enough with the saying to recognize it at once. More seriously, however, the potential *conflict* between the claims of God and the claims of earthly rulers is not the point under discussion in Romans 13:1-7, and the saying of Jesus is not sufficient for explaining the content of the exhortation in verse 7 or its relation to the statement in verse 6.

It could be argued, and many commentators have, that the exhortation to pay one's taxes as evidence of one's respectful subjection to the governing authorities has no particular problem in mind. Paul certainly did not have the kind of knowledge about the Roman congregation that he had about the one in Corinth. He had not founded the Roman church and had not yet been in Rome when he wrote this letter. The preceding exhortations in this section (12:3-21) are quite nonspecific and would be applicable to Christians anywhere. There are, in fact, similar admonitions in Paul's other letters. (A few examples: compare Rom. 12:3 with I Cor. 4:6, Rom. 12:10 with Phil. 2:3, Rom. 12:11-12 with I Thess. 5:16-19, Rom. 12:17 with I Thess. 5:15.) Must we not conclude, therefore, that the admonition to pay taxes is one more of these general illustrations of what it means to do God's will in one's daily life? Perhaps, but in this case there are two special points to consider. First, this is the *only* extant Pauline letter where the matter of taxes is raised. The payment of taxes is not a standard topic of Paul's moral instruction so far as our evidence allows us to judge. Second, the way this admonition is worded suggests that Paul does have a specific issue in mind, and one that he could have at least *supposed*, if he did not actually *know*, to be of concern to the Christians in Rome.

The distinctive wording of verse 7 is apparent as soon as we compare it with verse 6. One distinctive feature is of course the imperative mood; verse 7 is clearly an admonition, verse 6 is not. In the second place, verse 7 uses two different words to refer to taxes due, whereas verse 6 had used only one. One of these words (*phoros* in Greek) appears in both verses and is translated each time by "taxes" in the RSV. The second word (*telos* in Greek) appears only in verse 7, where the RSV has translated it as "revenue." Third, two different verbs are used in the two verses, although the RSV has used the same English word in each case. The distinction that is present in Greek is reflected in the NEB, however, where "pay" is used in verse 6 and "discharge" is used in verse 7. Finally, one is struck by the appearance of the word "all" in verse 7, where Paul charges his readers to hand over *to all* what is owed them.

What is the significance of these features of verse 7? The verb that NEB translates as "discharge" happens to be the same that is usually translated as "render" in Jesus' saying about Caesar and God. This has seemed to some a good indication that Paul is actually alluding to Jesus' saying in verse 7, but we have noted some reason to doubt this. There may be no special significance to the change of verbs. The other points, however, would be explained quite nicely if a recent suggestion by a team of German scholars can be accepted. Their whole argument need not be reproduced here, but in what follows I am dependent upon some important clues and conclusions they have presented.

In Paul's day the Roman government levied two main types of taxes, *direct* and *indirect*. It cannot be accidental that the two different words Paul uses for taxes in the passage before us are the Greek equivalents of the official Latin terms for those two types. The direct taxes (Latin: *tributa;* Greek: *phoros;* RSV: "taxes") were collected by government officials. The indirect taxes (Latin: *portoria;* Greek: *telos;* RSV: "revenue") were chiefly harbor fees and *ad valorem* duties on exports and imports. These were collected by companies of Roman knights, infamous for their abuse of the responsibility and their exploitation of the public. From the Roman historian Tacitus, we know that the public outrage at the corrupt practices of these citizen collectors of "revenues" reached a climax in A.D. 58. Tacitus reports that Nero, alarmed by the widespread unrest, seriously considered abolishing the indirect taxes altogether, as mindful as modern legislators that his popularity with the people would surely be increased! "His impulse, however," Tacitus goes on,

after much preliminary praise of his magnanimity, was checked by his older advisers, who pointed out that the dissolution of the empire was certain if the revenues on which the state subsisted were to be curtailed:—"For, the moment the duties on imports were removed, the logical sequel would be a demand for the abrogation of the direct taxes." (*Annals,* Book XIII, 50)

Nero did institute major reforms, however, issuing new regulations to govern the collection of the indirect taxes and waiving the right to trial of any collector caught abusing his office (Tacitus, *Annals,* Book XIII, 51).

Paul's letter to the Romans was written in A.D. 56 or 57, before Nero's tax reforms and during the period when public pressure was building against the abuses of the revenue collectors. Paul could not have been ignorant of this situation. Indeed, his mention in 13:4 of the one who "does not bear the sword in vain" might be a reference to special military police who were responsible for enforcing the collections of tax officials; the phrase Paul has employed matches the description of such police found in other ancient sources. Recent sociological studies of the Pauline congregations have demonstrated the probability that a significant number of the Apostle's own converts were persons of some means. These certainly did not constitute the majority in his congregations, but those congregations were not made up exclusively of the poor either. There were among them tradespeople, merchants, and others with substantial resources. These persons of the commercial class would have been exactly those most affected by the revenue abuses of the middle fifties.

If, now, we put together what is known about tax collections and tax problems in the early years of Nero's reign and what is known about the sociological makeup of Paul's congregations, we are able to read the injunction of Romans 13:7 with new appreciation. Paul would be urging his readers in Rome to pay all the taxes for which they were obligated (see "all of them" in verse 7). This would mean not only the direct taxes (*tributa*), which he could presume they would be paying anyway (verse 6), but also the controversial indirect ones (*portoria*). The Christians of Rome were in a strategic—and therefore sensitive—position. That had been proved some years earlier when their activity among the Jews of that city had precipitated the edict of Claudius (see above, page 105). We may suppose that one of the reasons Paul himself was eager to get to Rome (see, for example, Rom. 15:22-29) was his recognition of the importance for his own mission such a visit would have, indeed the specific help the Christians of Rome could give him in getting on to Spain (Rom. 15:24, 28). The factors that lie behind the admonition of 13:7 would then be as follows: (1) the present rising controversy about the justice of the revenue system of taxation; (2) the strategic location of the Christian congregation to whom Paul is writing; (3) the Apostle's own impending visit to the city, which he hopes will be beneficial to his ministry. In the meantime, Paul urges, pay whatever taxes are levied, without complaint. On the one hand, this will keep you safe from the punishment that, as God's servants, the government officials are authorized to administer and are known to administer through the "tax police." On the other hand, it is the wise and reasonable thing to do as a sign of your respect for law and order.

4. Summary

Our analysis of Romans 13:1-7, including the traditional views that are incorporated here, the literary-theological context in which it stands, and the specific issue to which it seems to be addressed, may be summed up as follows.

(1) The admonition to "be subject to the governing authorities" (verses 1 and 5) is secondary and preliminary to the main point of the passage, which is only disclosed in verses 6-7 (one should pay one's taxes in both kinds).

(2) Paul's view that the governing authorities have been appointed by God is not of his origination but is deeply rooted in the Jewish (particularly Hellenistic Jewish) tradition in which he stands.

(3) The traditional view includes the idea that earthly rulers function as God's servants, and that because the authority they

135

hold comes from God alone they are accountable to him for ruling wisely and benevolently.

(4) In Paul's day there had not yet been any fundamental confrontation between Rome and the church; the Empire could still be hailed as the one political force capable of creating and maintaining political, economic, and social stability in the world; and the young Nero (only nineteen or twenty years of age when Paul wrote this letter) showed promise of being a just emperor.

(5) Paul does not believe the tax issue is one in which the Christians of Rome should become embroiled; they should demonstrate their support of the rule of law by paying whatever taxes are levied.

Conclusion

Our examination of Romans 13:1-7 was prompted by the question whether this passage does not in fact contradict the otherwise clear Pauline principle that Christians are in the world but not of it. As we have analyzed the passage, its special pertinence for Paul and his readers has become increasingly evident. This requires us to pose a second question, however: To the extent that we are able to affirm the particular relevance of Romans 13:1-7 for Paul and the Roman Christians in A.D. 56–57, are we not simultaneously diminishing its relevance for Christians two thousand years later, facing immensely different and more complex political realities? In answer to the first question, we may respond that Romans 13:1-7 is not only compatible with Paul's own principle but, read in its context and against the background we have sketched, actually illustrates that principle. The considerations that allow us to arrive at this conclusion may be formulated in several points, which, taken together, constitute a response to the second question as well: There are some fundamental ways in which this passage may still speak to us today.

1. *Authority is not to be considered an intrinsic property of those by whom it is exercised.* Paul's way of saying this is that "there is no authority except from God" (13:1*b*). The authority of the governing powers is something with which they have been entrusted. It is surprising that this point, basic to the whole argument of the passage, has so often been overlooked. The authors of the American Declaration of Independence were called revolutionaries for claiming something similar, although, to be sure, they approached the matter rather differently. Governments derive "their just powers from the consent of the governed," they wrote; and, thus authorized, the government has a duty to secure for its citizens those "unalienable rights" with which all people "are endowed by their Creator." Paul does not and could not speak of "the consent of the governed." Whether he *would* have spoken this way had the political realities of his day been different is moot. However, the conviction that he shares with his religious tradition and that he affirms in Romans 13:1-7 is in its own way a "declaration of independence" from any earthly power that would claim to exercise a self-generated and self-validating authority. That the practical political consequences of this are nowhere indicated by the Apostle may be due in part to the relatively favorable political situation that obtained during his ministry. It is due most of all, however, to his belief that all earthly institutions are in the process of "passing away."

2. *The governing authorities are accountable to God.* If Romans 13:1-7 may be seen as a Christian "declaration of independence" from all tyrannical governments, it may also be seen as a declaration of the *dependence* of all earthly rulers upon God. Since their authority has been given to them, they are dependent upon and accountable to the One from whom it has come. Paul here specifically describes the government author-ities as the "servants" and "ministers" of God. The authority they exercise has its basis in this relationship, and from this belief

it is but a step to the conclusion that when they no longer exercise authority in God's service it is no longer the authority of God. But what is their proper function? Paul is explicit about this.

3. *The governing authorities exist to serve "the good" of those who are governed.* They can be said to be exercising the authority given them by God when they support those who do good and restrain those who do evil (Rom. 13:3-4*a*). They are responsible for the rule of law in society, for the administration of justice. One may describe this function according to the context of Romans 12 and 13 as: the maintenance of an ordered society wherein God's will may be sought out and obeyed. It is important to observe that Paul does *not* regard the governing authorities as agents of "salvation." He envisions no Utopia, no perfect society, no theocracy, no "Christian government." The function of the governing authorities is important, but it is not all-embracing; and it belongs still and only to the old age, which is passing away. The Roman Empire, no matter how chastened, will not become God's kingdom; no Caesar, however noble, will be God's Messiah. Just as Paul declines to regard authority as an intrinsic property of government, so also he declines to regard the governing authorities as inherently either good or evil. They are appointed to *support* the good, but they are not themselves the arbiters of what is good.

4. *The Christian's "subjection" to the governing authorities is secondary to his or her obedience to the will of God.* The whole context within which Romans 13:1-7 stands, as well as what the passage itself says about the authority, accountability, and specific function of the governing authorities, points to this conclusion. The opening appeal in Romans 12:1-2 reminds the readers that their lives are not to be patterned after this present age; as transformed persons they are to seek God's will and do what is acceptable in his sight. Similarly, the closing summary and appeals remind the readers that they stand finally only under the "law" of love (13:8-10) and that they belong not to

the "night" of this present age, but finally only to the "day" (13:11-13). Their Lord is not Caesar, but Jesus Christ (13:14). Here we are in touch with the fundamental Pauline principle that Christians belong to another "commonwealth" and that their ultimate allegiance is to God. This point is not repealed or compromised by anything Paul says in Romans 13:1-7. He does not say or imply that Christians belong to their rulers in any ultimate sense. He makes it clear that those rulers are themselves dependent upon God and exist to serve what may be reckoned good according to God's will. His reference to the role of "conscience," verse 5, is crucial. Not only the external restraints and sanctions of the governing authorities, but also one's own critical reflection and judgment about what is "good" come into play. There is no need for Paul to develop the point, of course, because in the case before him he sees no conflict between the Christian's conscience and the law's requirements.

Neither Romans 13:1-7 nor the other problem texts we have examined should be used as sacred cows or discarded as white elephants. Their special pertinence to the conditions and needs of the first century precludes the first, whereas the fundamental theological and moral concerns that lie behind them preclude the second. In summarizing and concluding the admonitions of Romans 12 and 13, Paul reminds us that those who are committed to finding and doing God's will should have only one debt, but it is a constant one—to love. In effect, the concrete ethical teaching of Paul requires us to reformulate every question about our life in the world into the question about our common life before God. It requires us to understand that faith is not faith until it is enacted in love. And it requires us to find out what this means concretely, given the realities of our own place and time, and to do it.

139

For Further Reading

On the general topic of this chapter see the article, "Rome, Early Christian Attitudes Toward," by Gerhard Krodel in *The Interpreter's Dictionary of the Bible,* Vol. 5, which has a brief bibliography. Two essays by Ernst Käsemann provide an excellent orientation to the context and underlying issues of Romans 13:1-7, "Worship and Everyday Life: A Note on Romans 12," and "Principles of the Interpretation of Romans 13," both in *New Testament Questions of Today* (Philadelphia: Fortress Press, 1969).

In the present chapter, I have relied on several of the basic insights of an article coauthored by three German scholars, Johannes Friedrich, Wolfgang Pöhlmann, and Peter Stuhlmacher. This is an exceedingly thorough study of the historical situation and intention of Romans 13:1-7, but it is so far available only in German, in the *Zeitschrift für Theologie und Kirche,* 73, 1976, pages 131-66. Abraham J. Malherbe's *Social Aspects of Early Christianity* (Baton Rouge: Louisiana State University Press, 1977) provides an introduction to some recent social-historical analyses of the Pauline congregations, and makes the point that there were some persons of considerable means within them. If so, then the possibility is increased that Romans 13:1-7 reflects the controversies about the revenue system known to have occurred under Nero.

The Loeb Classical Library has again been used where possible to quote ancient sources: Josephus, *The Jewish War,* trans. H. St. J. Thackeray (1927); Philo, *On the Embassy to Gaius,* trans. F. H. Colson (1962); Tacitus, *Annals,* trans. John Jackson (1937). The *Letter of Aristeas* is quoted from the translation of H. T. Andrews in R. H. Charles, *The Apocrypha and Pseudepigrapha of the Old Testament in English,* Vol. II (Oxford: At the Clarendon Press, 1913). The saying of Rabbi Hanina is cited by G. F. Moore in his discussion of "Duties to

Rulers," pages 112-18 in *Judaism in the First Centuries of the Christian Era,* Vol. II (Cambridge: Harvard University Press, 1932).

J. C. O'Neill is quoted from his commentary, *Paul's Letter to the Romans* (Baltimore: Penguin Books, 1975), p. 209. O'Neill himself believes that Romans 13:1-7 is not Pauline, and he makes similar judgments (unpersuasive to most) about large portions of Romans. In addition to Käsemann's commentary on Romans noted at the end of chapter 3, see C. E. B. Cranfield, *A Commentary on Romans 12–13,* "Scottish Journal of Theology Occasional Papers," 12 (Edinburgh: Oliver and Boyd, 1965), and the treatment of Romans 13:1-7 in J. H. Yoder, *The Politics of Jesus* (Grand Rapids: Eerdmans, 1972), chapter 10.

Index of Scripture Passages
(Selected)

Genesis
1:27 — 99-100
2:18-23 — 99, 100, 101
2:24 — 35, 48
19:1-28 — 54-57

Leviticus
18:3-4 — 64
18:22 — 58, 63-64
19:4, 19 — 64
20:13 — 58, 63-64

Deuteronomy
23:17 — 54

Judges
19:1-26 — 55

I Kings
14:24 — 54
15:12 — 54, 58
22:46 — 54

II Kings
23:7 — 54

Ezekiel
16:47-50 — 56

Matthew
5:31-32 — 40
10:15 — 56
11:23-24 — 56
19:9 — 40

Mark
10:11-12 — 40
12:17 — 131, 133

Luke
10:12 — 56
16:18 — 40

Acts
16:11-15, 40 — 104
18:1-26 — 105-8
23:16 — 102

Romans
1:18-32 — 74-78, 81-82, 120
1:26-27 — 58, 68, 73-78, 79-81
3:22b-23 — 74
5:6-11 — 26, 82, 125
12:1-2 — 23-24, 116, 123, 125, 126, 138
13:1-7 — 115, 117-39
13:8-14 — 23-24, 123, 125

16:1-2	108-10
16:3-5	106-7
16:3-16	110
16:8	109

I Corinthians

5:1-13	70-71
6:1 ff	13, 71, 117, 129
6:9	54, 58, 68-71, 73
6:9-11	70
6:12-13	32, 33
6:15-16	34, 35
7	30, 32-50, 89
7:1	31, 33
7:2-7	33-38
7:7a	13
7:8	103
7:8-9	38-39, 41
7:10	131
7:10-11	39-43
7:12-16	43-46
7:28	37
7:29-31	37, 38, 116
7:32-34	37
7:35	37, 49
7:36-38	38-39, 103
9:5	102
10:23	32, 33
11:2-16	92, 95-102, 111
11:11	35
11:14-15	13, 80
12:13	93, 94
14:33b-36	85, 86, 91-92, 118
16:19	106

Galatians

| 3:27-28 | 92-95, 101, 102, 111-12 |

| 5:6 | 22, 26 |
| 6:2 | 13, 125 |

Ephesians

| 5:21-33 | 47-48, 89 |
| 5:22-24 | 89-91 |

Philippians

3:19	116
3:20	24, 116
3:21	116-17
4:2-3	104-5

Colossians

| 3:11 | 93 |
| 3:18 | 41, 48, 89-91 |

I Thessalonians

| 4:3b-5 | 34 |
| 4:4-5 | 48, 49 |

I Timothy

1:10	57, 58, 71-72
2:8-15	87-89
2:11-12	108
3:16	14, 15

Philemon

| 2 | 110 |

I Peter

| 2:17 | 128 |

Jude

| 6, 7 | 56 |

143